MW01282704

THE LEGAL BASIS
for a MORAL
CONSTITUTION

A GUIDE FOR CHRISTIANS
TO UNDERSTAND AMERICA'S
CONSTITUTIONAL CRISIS

JENNA ELLIS, ESQ.

Foreword by Michael Farris, J.D., LL.M.

WESTBOW
PRESS®
A DIVISION OF THOMAS NELSON
& ZONDERVAN

WestBow Press books may be ordered through booksellers or by contacting:

WestBow Press
A Division of Thomas Nelson & Zondervan
1663 Liberty Drive
Bloomington, IN 47403
www.westbowpress.com
1 (866) 928-1240

ISBN: 978-1-5127-2275-8 (sc)
ISBN: 978-1-5127-2276-5 (hc)
ISBN: 978-1-5127-2274-1 (e)

Library of Congress Control Number: 2015920353

Print information available on the last page.

WestBow Press rev. date: 12/22/2015

CONTENTS

To Jesus Christ,
My Advocate

&

To My Family,
My Parents, Dave & Valerie,
My Brothers, David and Tyler,

All of whom I love with all my heart

CRITICAL ACCLAIM:
WHAT CHRISTIAN THINKERS ARE
SAYING ABOUT THIS BOOK!

"Well-written, easy to read, full of good information and explanation that the average American just does not know. This book will be a good reference for the Christian perspective of how our government works and where the flash points of conflict arise. I love the way Jenna Ellis keeps going to worldview foundations. Her work will engender lots of discussion and good debate. This is exactly the kind of resource we can use with the Colson Center."

Dr. William Brown
Senior Fellow for Worldview and Culture
The Chuck Colson Center for Christian Worldview

"Jenna Ellis has written a masterful book providing a foundation for the basic principle that all law is based in someone's morality. The question becomes, whose morality was intended by America's Founders? This is an important question for America today as our nation moves away from its foundations in the morality recognized by the Founders to a new morality that turns 180 degrees away from the Founders' basic moral premise. The ultimate question then becomes whether America can survive uprooted from its original moral foundations."

David Gibbs III, Esq.
President, National Center for Life and Liberty
Author, 'Understanding the Constitution'

"Given that those in power depend greatly on 'low information voters' and the 'stupidity of the American voter,' it is all the more imperative that citizens, and especially Christians and the Church, do their homework, be responsible for informing themselves, and know about their country and how it works. Jenna Ellis has provided an excellent, step-by-step overview of the Constitution's call for biblical morality, how court decisions have, over the past 60 years, eroded that call, and how we can effectively engage our system of government to renew within it the Judeo-Christian worldview our nation was founded upon."

Nancy Pearcey
Professor at Houston Baptist University
Author of 'Total Truth' and 'Finding Truth'

"As a lawyer, Jenna Ellis offers fresh insights into the legal purpose of the founding documents. These do not contain mere philosophical musings. Instead, the Declaration of Independence and the Constitution were penned by lawyers, using legal terminology, and they provided the legal rationale and effected the legal founding of the United States. Ellis argues that the founding documents grounded their legitimacy in Divine Law, not in any form of social contract theory, which means that they cannot legitimately be turned into "fluid" documents at the whim of current judges. Throughout, Ellis

provides fascinating insights into what the founders really meant—
and what they should mean for us today."

Frank Peretti
Best-selling author of 'This Present Darkness' and 'The Oath'

"At a time in our nation where basic concepts of freedom and
liberty are being re-imagined and re-defined, Jenna Ellis provides
a timely and helpful exploration of 'why law and what law' against
a rapidly changing cultural landscape. As an attorney, Jenna's
examination of the Founders as lawyers presents a fresh and
insightful perspective to our nation's origins and its implications
for today. Her discussion reaches beyond the typical historical,
legal narrative, analyzing the critical role of human desire for
validation and the proper role of a legal system in reflecting that
universal craving.

As a millennial, it is encouraging to see someone from our generation
give a practical overview of our legal system while tackling the grey
that is driving it. Regardless of where one falls on the hot-button
issues of our day, Jenna's book is a helpful tool in examining our past
in order to move towards a hopeful and vast future."

Kerri Kupec
Legal Communications Director
Alliance Defending Freedom

"When five unelected, unregenerate judges of the Supreme Court
shook their fists at almighty God and redefined His mandate for
marriage, it signaled a dogmatic departure from the God-ordained
objective morality our country once embraced. Jenna Ellis's book is
a timely one and provides much-needed insight into the legal reasons
our nation must return to objective moral judgments that were

established by our God and Creator in His Word. Morality should never be viewed as a changing standard dictated by the majority of our Supreme Court Justices. I highly recommend Jenna Ellis and her excellent work in *The Legal Basis for a Moral Constitution!*"

Mike Gendron, M.A.B.S.
Dallas Theological Seminary
Director, Proclaiming the Gospel Ministry

"Most Americans are instinctively aware that something is desperately wrong with today's legal system. Yet, very few are able to explain why or pinpoint the actual reason for the problem. America's founding documents were not created in a philosophical vacuum. Rather, a deep and vast moral, theological, and biblical worldview provided the backdrop for America's foundation and experiment in self-government. It remains impossible to understand America's underpinnings independent of this accompanying worldview. As was true in Josiah's day before the re-discovery of God's neglected Law in the Temple (2 Kings 22), it's all too easy for a nation to lose sight of its own history. Yet, when this history is obscured or lost, a nation's founding institutions will remain an enigma to contemporary observers.

Fortunately, in this book, attorney and committed Christian Jenna Ellis brings to light the true worldview behind America's foundation. In so doing, she provides much needed illumination in helping explain both the Declaration of Independence and the U.S. Constitution. She not only clarifies to the reader what these foundational documents actually mean, but she also provides the necessary steps toward restoring them to their original purpose. Anyone who is concerned about America's current political and legal drift and what can be done to restore America to her proper foundation will be interested in Jenna Ellis's research and writing."

Dr. Andy Woods, J.D., Ph.D.

Professor of Bible and Theology at the College of Biblical Studies in Houston, TX
Senior Pastor of Sugar Land Bible Church, Sugar Land, TX

"Ms. Ellis offers us a clear, needed, and compelling analysis of the moral basis of our Constitution. In a time of moral decay and legal anarchy, this philosophical, cultural, and legal analysis is a tonic to the illogic and destructiveness of secular thought. I recommend that all concerned citizens read it, especially law students, lawyers, politicians, and judges."

Dr. Douglas Groothuis

Professor of Philosophy, Denver Seminary
Author of 'Christian Apologetics: A Comprehensive Case for Biblical Faith'

The well-known 19th Century German atheist Friedrich Nietzsche once remarked, "I fear we are not getting rid of God because we still believe in grammar." Nietzsche evidently understood what many people today do not: words matter. Language is foundational to all of life. Indeed, in the beginning God *spoke* the world into existence. Nietzsche knew that if you eliminate the concepts of *original meaning* and *authorial intent* from language, the result will be a world where words no longer have meaning and chaos ensues.

In her new book, *The U. S. Constitution and the Bible*, Jenna Ellis has done a masterful job of demonstrating the vital importance of holding fast to these foundational concepts by drawing crucial parallels between the interpretation the Bible and the interpretation of God's Word. As believers, we ignore the plain, normal, original meaning of the Bible to our peril. And as a nation, deviating from the Founding Fathers' plain, normal, original meaning of the Constitution will undoubtedly lead to the destruction of our nation.

J. B. Hixson, Ph.D.
President, Not By Works Ministries

"Men and women of all ages will benefit greatly by reading *The Legal Basis for a Moral Constitution*. We rarely think of the Declaration of Independence and the Constitution as moral and spiritual documents. But Justice Joseph Story rightly said, 'The rights of conscience are beyond the just reach of any human power. They are given by God, and cannot be encroached upon by human authority without criminal disobedience of the precepts of natural as well as of revealed religion.'"

Pastor Gino Geraci
Salem Media Talk Show Host
Law Enforcement Chaplain

ACKNOWLEDGEMENTS

This book would not have been possible without the extraordinary mentorship and guidance of several key players in the constitutional law arena and in the battleground of worldviews and philosophy.

I am particularly indebted to Michael Farris for his investment in this project and also in me as a constitutional attorney. That someone of his caliber would take the time for mentorship is a testament to his sincere love of law and love of Christ. It is incredibly inspiring to have a real-life hero to look up to and strive to be like.

I am also exceedingly grateful for Nancy Pearcey, whose worldview education through the World Journalism Institute provided me with the framework to understand the law from a biblical perspective. Her friendship, encouragement, and sound advice are treasured.

I am grateful for the blessing of my pastor, Gino Geraci, who has taught me through example what it actually means to speak truth in love, and my church family, for their faithful prayers and enthusiasm. I am thankful for the extended pastoral care of Paul Van Noy, Mike Gendron, and Tim Remington.

I am also thankful for Tim G. Echols and his influence in my life. Through his faithfulness following God's calling in his own life, his ministry provided the mechanism for God to show me my calling in law at the young age of 14. God continues to use him mightily to influence the next generation.

So many people contributed their advice, encouragement, and prayers to this book that it would be impossible to name them all, and I appreciate that each one took the time to care about this project.

I was fortunate to receive help in legal and grammatical editing from my friend and colleague Matthew Hegarty, whose contributions to better my writing over the years have been significant. I am thankful for his generous offer of assistance.

I am honored to be a proud alumna of the University of Richmond T.C. Williams School of Law, which provided me with the best possible legal education and academic environment to learn. I grew in my passion for the philosophy and practice of law and advocacy because of Richmond Law and its dedicated faculty. I am eternally grateful to Deans Michelle L. Rahman and W. Clark Williams, Jr. for being my advocates and Dean Emeritus John G. Douglass for his mentorship during my law school tenure and the opportunities he provided to me to learn the craft of lawyering.

Finally, I am overwhelmingly thankful to my parents and my brothers for their love, support, and prayers throughout this year especially and throughout the course of my life. God placed me within the most wonderful family anyone could ever have and I am so happy to be their daughter and sister. Thank you, Mom and Dad, for always championing my calling in law and your faithful support of this book.

FOREWORD

In 1988, I was part of a small delegation to the Soviet Union, which was led by Congressman Frank Wolf. Our mission was to advocate for religious liberty in the USSR—especially on behalf of Christians and Jews, who were the primary targets of repression.

While we met as a group with a variety of Soviet officials, I was dispatched by myself to visit with a group of lawyers who were rewriting the Soviet constitution. It was an effort to prop up the USSR in the last days before its eventual crash. My goal was to urge these constitutional revisionists to include religious freedom for parents to allow them to bring their children to church and to offer them religious education as an alternative to public schools.

When I made the request to the lawyers in the room, they replied, "What international document recognizes such rights?"

At the time, I didn't know all that much about international law documents. Since then, I have earned an LLM in Public International Law from the University of London. And my answer today would have included citations from the Universal Declaration of Human Rights, the International Covenant on Civil and Political Rights, and the International Covenant on Economic Social and Cultural Rights.

But the answer I gave them was this: "I don't know whether any international law documents protect such rights, but the moral law of God clearly does so. Parents have the inherent right to direct the religious training and education of their children."

Their chairman replied, "You need to remember that we are Communists and do not accept God as a premise for law."

Human rights are a difficult concept if one begins with atheism as a premise. In fact, it was one of the earliest articles in my LLM course that more clearly elucidated this challenge. The author posed the question, *Why are concepts of human rights universal in character?* His article wrestled with the fact that if human rights ideals are merely created by men, then why is it that people from nearly every nation have such similar constructs of the theory of human rights?

The article explored every man-based theory of human rights and the author systematically demonstrated that no theory accounted for the universal nature of the theory. In the end, he concluded that only Christianity—the original source of human rights theory—presented an internally consistent defense of the universality of human rights. However, he said, since Christianity was nothing more than fairy stories, then this fails as an explanation despite its logical consistency. Thus, human rights are universal, but no one knows why.

This is true. No one who rejects God as a premise for human rights law can explain why principles are universal and should be universal.

All law has a foundation that dramatically influences the ultimate content and contours of the legal system that is built thereon. Why should we have self-government? Why is freedom better than a dictatorship? Why is limited government better than an all-powerful central government? These and a myriad of other questions are directly influenced by the foundations upon which a system of law and government are built.

My belief in the principle of self-government is built on my understanding of the nature of man as a creature of God—explained and buttressed by specific passages of Scripture (such as Deuteronomy 17:14 *et seq.* and Hosea 8:1–4). But I don't believe that self-government is best just for Christians or westerners. Since God has created all men in His image, then self-government is the best form of government for all people of all nations. And since God has created the human soul to desire freedom, self-government can only be born of freedom and not by external coercion.

I offer these thoughts not to try to explain my entire philosophy of law and government, but to give a sufficient example to explain why one's foundational assumptions about God and man directly influence one's philosophy of law and government. Some books try to teach us facts. Other books try to teach us theories that the author wants us to accept. Jenna Ellis will teach you some facts. She will also teach you some theories of law and government that she believes deeply and thinks that you and our nation will benefit from greatly if you join her in sharing these beliefs. But, Jenna also does something more and something that is exceedingly rare.

She makes her arguments in a way that models critical thinking and philosophical analysis. You will often hear schools claim that they don't want to teach children what to think, but how to think. In my experience, such schools are the exception rather than the rule. Like teachers, authors who teach you how to think are operating at the top end of the craft.

Jenna Ellis marshals facts, law, and history to make a clear defense of the theory that American law was created with the premise that Divine Law (God-given, objective moral law) is the ultimate standard of both truth and justice. Since she was my student in constitutional law, there would be some temptation to conclude that she got all of these theories from my class. That would be a mistaken conclusion.

Jenna went on to law school and legal practice and has done something few lawyers ever even attempt. She has written a full defense of the

Christian worldview as the proper basis for law. As a teacher, I always tell my students that they do not have to agree with my theories to do well on their assignments. I grade them on how well they defend their own theories.

I am extremely proud of Jenna. She has written a thought-provoking book. It is well worth reading. You will learn from it as I have learned from it. You, like me, don't have to agree with every jot and tittle to recognize that this is one of the finest defenses of Christian legal theory of our era.

The Soviet lawyers I met in 1988 said it well. A nation's law proceeds from its premises. If we start with God, there is a clear path to freedom and justice. If we start with man as the measure of all things, the path is troubled and dangerous and will never achieve the goals of human rights and freedom that indeed burn within the soul of every person on earth.

Michael Farris, J.D., LL.M.
Chancellor
Patrick Henry College

"We have no government armed with power capable of contending with human passions unbridled by morality and religion. Our Constitution was made only for a moral and religious people. It is wholly inadequate to the government of any other."[1]

- John Adams

INTRODUCTION

WHY AMERICANS STILL CARE ABOUT MORALITY AND THE U.S. CONSTITUTION

I started writing this book well before the *Obergefell v. Hodges*[2] same-sex marriage decision was handed down in June 2015. That Supreme Court opinion simply further necessitated a comprehensive, logical, and legal argument for a moral basis to Constitutional interpretation. In the aftermath of that decision, the States and the American people in general were left in a Constitutional crisis greater than we have ever faced since the original Constitutional Convention in 1787.

As Americans, we are adrift in a huge, murky melting pot of so many different ideas, cultures, faiths, and worldviews that we have largely embraced the mantra that in order to safely coexist, no one can or should assert any moral conclusions. That, the secularists argue, would be imposing my views on you, which absolutely cannot be tolerated in the name of absolute tolerance. Liberty, they argue, can only be asserted when it is not offensive to anyone else. Free speech and possessing sincerely held beliefs and values have become "bigotry."

With the rise of modern social media, expert opinion has become vastly watered down so that any person's opinion, whether fact-based, informed or not, or merely a reflexive reaction based on personal experience or emotion, can be published and unleashed on the world. And of course, any person's opinion must be tolerated and accepted, so long as the opinion itself is tolerant and acceptable.

The 24/7 cycle of noise and chattering opinion has so muddied the waters that our society is both harshly critical of any "hating" or "bigoted" opinion that differs from one's own and also firmly demanding complete tolerance for everyone's opinion—simultaneously.

We are in a cultural crisis also.

Yet within this pool of raging inconsistencies, the general public still understands why objective, authoritative justification matters—not just having support for an opinion from friends and family or the latest poll showing the majority opinion currently agrees with one's own stance. We still want authoritative *validation*.

The so-called "same-sex marriage" decision, *Obergefell*, was a key example of this social paradox. Most of the LGBT response and celebration was not about legalization, government benefits, or the same-sex community's satisfaction in a slight majority on the Supreme Court currently favoring their cause, but rather it focused on the idea that their same-sex couplings (and by theoretical extension, polyamorous and other "unions") were finally validated by the highest government authority and therefore considered just as *valuable* as heterosexual unions. A government license equals government value and validation.

Even the final paragraph of the opinion, written by Justice Kennedy and the portion most widely reposted on social media, discussed this very *moral* value judgment:

> "No union is more profound than marriage, for it embodies the highest ideals of love, fidelity, devotion, sacrifice, and family. In forming a marital union,

two people become something greater than they once were. As some of the petitioners in these cases demonstrate, marriage embodies a love that may endure even past death. It would misunderstand these men and women to say they disrespect the idea of marriage. Their plea is that they do respect it, respect it so deeply that they seek to find its fulfillment for themselves. Their hope is not to be condemned to live in loneliness, excluded from one of civilization's oldest institutions. ***They ask for equal dignity in the eyes of the law***"[3] (emphasis added).

In other words, the LGBT community asked for a value judgment and moral validation from the Supreme Court, via (supposedly) the U.S. Constitution.

This is a fascinating insight into the American psyche and the current mantra's contradiction. Jean-Paul Sartre, secular existentialist philosopher, wrote, "[Man] was free, free in every way, free to behave like a fool or a machine, free to accept, free to refuse, free to equivocate; to marry, to give up the game, to drag this death weight about with him for years to come. He could do what he liked, no one had the right to advise him, there would be for him no Good or Evil unless he thought them into being."[4]

But if we are truly free, independent beings that have broken free from the "bonds" of social custom or of anyone else's judgment and live only within our own reality, as secularists like Sartre assert, why should we care about the law's value judgment or morality at all?

We care because we are still human beings with a conscience, and as much as we try to intellectually liberate ourselves from any bonds of nature or social or government-imposed "labels" on gender, race, sexual orientation, traditional family composition, marriage, morality, etc., we still know objective morality and value exists outside of ourselves. And we still crave its validation.

As much as we may preach tolerance and equality of all opinions, every person understands the difference between simply holding an opinion ourselves and having that opinion legitimized and validated through the law or an actual authority. Winning a civil lawsuit or securing a criminal trial acquittal turns a person's *claim* of damages or innocence into a *legitimate* legal result.

The law as a whole is an expression of what a society values and its morality. Our justice system shows that we value due process and the right to a fair trial. We value protecting life and liberty. The law is our codified morality, expressed through our formal authorization on everything from what acts we criminally punish to what we allow science to test in petri dishes and on animals.

The law is, and always has been, used to impose a specific worldview on culture. We cannot escape the fact that law is therefore always inherently moral.

This is why we care about things like abortion laws. Both sides argue from a value-based premise: one side values the life of the unborn child, the other side values the mother's choice over whether to keep or destroy the life of the unborn child. But make no mistake— both sides argue and appeal to morality and to the inalienable right of humanity, and both sides seek to have their values legitimized through the law's inherent authority.

The law carries a distinct, intrinsic aspect of legitimacy and authority. We can all relate to the old Western movies' display of this inherent power and real authority in the law, and when the sheriff said, "I am the Law," even children know there is an immediate air of respect for that authority. The Law was in town to straighten things out and bring justice to the people. My brothers and I grew up playing "cops and robbers" and we knew that the cops were the "good guys" and the robbers were the "bad guys." This is a simple example of a value judgment where even children understand basic morality—good versus bad, right versus wrong. We all know from an early age that legal authority is inherently moral and valuable.

The *Obergefell* decision was celebrated because the law had provided a *value* judgment on the morality of same-sex marriage, not just a (supposedly) morally neutral legalization of homosexual activity—such legalization had already occurred in 2003 in the *Lawrence v. Texas* decision when the Court struck down sodomy laws, making same-sex sexual activity legal under a fabricated "privacy right" found nowhere in the U.S. Constitution. In *Obergefell*, the Supreme Court went further. Now, the highest Court in the United States told the LGBT community that their homosexual lifestyle was not just legal privately, but morally validated openly through government recognition and social celebration and therefore equally as valued as heterosexual unions.

Of course, the opinions raged back and forth for decades prior to *Obergefell*, but because the Court validated same-sex marriage, the LGBT community now believes it has the moral ground to assert equal value of same-sex unions. Prior to June 26, 2015, the LGBT community demanded only absolute tolerance for its viewpoints and lifestyle. After *Obergefell*, the community demanded absolute celebration and *value* and believes it possesses moral authority to insist upon that value.

The celebration extended beyond private LGBT couplings into mainstream companies lauding the decision as a moral validation. Posts appeared on Twitter the morning of the decision, lauding the moral aspect of the judgment with the hashtag #loveislove and statements like "Celebrating marriage equality!" and "Love is Love! Now no one can tell you otherwise."

These posts by such major corporations also appeared to be part of a larger, overall marketing device to integrate themselves with the LGBT community and appear "progressive" and "tolerant" via the celebration.

As one writer determined, "Legal gay marriage is not the endgame for the gay-rights movement. It never was. **Moral approval** is the endgame. The agenda is not tolerance for different beliefs and lifestyles. The agenda is a demand that everyone get on board with the **moral revolution** or be punished. That means if you or your church won't get with the program, then the revolutionaries will endeavor to close you down"[6] (emphasis added).

If members of the progressive secular community were actually consistent with their amoral worldview—that there is no absolute universal morality existing in reality and that nothing matters but their own individual opinions and independent value judgments— they would be indifferent to whether or not the government legitimized their opinions. They would have been perfectly content with the privacy of their own reality.

But Americans still understand value and how our law imposes that morality on the whole. We still place a great deal of weight to our Constitutional authority and what our laws choose to say about us and our national moral compass. But if we actually cannot divorce law from moral judgments, whose morality is really controlling and whose morality is *legitimate* authority?

This book offers insight into the legal reasons our nation must be compelled to return to universally objective moral judgments from a higher source than the collective government. Morality is not the subjective, changing whim of the majority, or more specifically, the majority of nine Supreme Court Justices. It will unpack a comprehensive, logical, and legal argument for the only legitimate basis of objective morality within the U.S. Constitution, through its history and foundations, and then provide a proposed solution: the Article V Convention of States project.

We will first look at the problem of morality in our secularized culture, and expand on this basic premise that regardless of how insistent the modern culture is that morality is a matter of personal belief, it is actually a necessarily objective component of law. Chapter 1 sets the big-picture framework for our analysis of morality within the government.

But we still have to go back to the Founders at the inception of this argument and understand their relationship with the law, not just morality. Chapter 2 answers the question: Does the faith of the Founding Fathers matter? Much of the modern era moral debate centers solely on this question, but we will take the argument into a new area, showing why we can be certain of an objective, fixed interpretation of the U.S. Constitution on a legal basis other than the Founders' personal faith.

Understanding who the Founders were is a good start, but it is only the beginning. We must unpack what they knew about the authority of law and government itself. We also must understand and process the basic concepts central to American jurisprudence contemporaneous to the Founders. Chapter 3 provides an overview of the Founding Documents as *legal* documents, and also shows the foundation of authority for American government as a whole.

This concept sets up Chapter 4, which shows that the U.S. Constitution is at the top of a carefully, purposefully designed Founding Documents Hierarchy and that the U.S. Constitution cannot be wholly understood and interpreted *per ipsum*, divorced from the roots and the foundation it was built upon.

The question of proper interpretation of text is also necessary to understand the Founding Documents. Correct interpretation is essential to deriving rightful meaning. Chapter 5 provides five key principles for Constitutional interpretation.

Chapters 6–8 unpack and analyze the actual text of the Founding Documents one by one, and, through the lens of the law, show the plain meaning of the legal documents significant to American government—The Declaration of Independence, the Federalist Papers, and the U.S. Constitution.

With that grounding in contemporaneous U.S. Constitutional history and the plain meaning of the Founding Documents, we then turn to subsequent Constitutional history, post-1789. Chapter 9 deals with the two main theories of Constitutional interpretation: Judicial Activism and Judicial Restraint.

Chapter 10 presents nine specific examples of Constitutional case studies and shows exactly where the Supreme Court has twisted and changed the original meaning of the U.S. Constitution through an assertion of legal fiction—ideas and legal doctrines nowhere in true, valid meaning of the U.S. Constitution. We will look at the worldview assumptions underpinning these Constitutional Law cases and see how the Supreme Court has systematically attempted to replace the firm foundations of law with amoral doctrines.

Because we will see that moral law is an inherently necessary component of correct interpretation of Constitutional text, Chapter 11 will further illustrate why moral law is by definition objective and from a higher source than man's agreement. Following a C.S. Lewis argument for objective moral law, we will contemplate why we can be certain of moral law's objective existence and application.

The issue of religious freedom is of paramount concern to Christians, churches, and faith-based organizations in the midst of this constitutional crisis. Understanding the real meaning of the First Amendment and where our religious freedom rights are derived is critical to preserving these rights and our free exercise. Chapter 12 discusses religious freedom in the context of the Founders' intent and the current secular push to prioritize "equality" and other so-called rights over actual rights, including religious freedom.

Finally, we will face the ultimate question: what can we do now? As constitutional attorney Michael Farris suggests, our Founders gave us Article V for such a time as this. He and a growing number of other legal constitutional scholars are advancing the solution as an Article V Convention of States. Chapter 13 will dive deeper into the Convention of States proposal and how this may be the best, legally viable solution that the Founders themselves would have proposed and for which they actually provided through Article V of the U.S. Constitution.

It is my sincere desire to educate and edify the body of Christ through this book, and it was with that passion that this book was inspired. Psalm 119 is entirely about the psalmist David's passion for law. My hope is that this book will ignite that passion for law in the reader and bring clarity to the Christian's argument for moral law in society. I hope the reader will be encouraged to stand firm in Truth and emboldened to speak that Truth in love.

Jenna Lynn Ellis, Esq.
Denver, Colorado
October 16, 2015

CHAPTER 1

PROGRESSIVE GOVERNMENT'S BIGGEST PROBLEM: MORALITY

"The human understanding is a revelation from its Maker, which can never be disputed or doubted. There can be no skepticism…or incredulity or infidelity here. No prophecies, no miracles are necessary to prove this celestial communication. This revelation has been made certain that two and one make three, and that one is not three nor can three be one. We can never be so certain…as we are from the revelation of nature, that is, nature's God, that two and two are equal to four."[7]

- John Adams

The question that has plagued both the judiciary and every well-informed citizen centers on interpretation of the U.S. Constitution. By this, I mean the interpretation of the written text of the U.S. Constitution, not the 225 years of Supreme Court opinions that have attempted to interpret that text.

This is an important distinction at the outset, because if we begin with the presumption that Constitutional interpretation includes the Supreme Court opinions, then we assume that each of these opinions has already been determined to correctly interpret the actual text.

One of the significant problems with the way Constitutional Law is taught in law schools today is that law schools take Supreme Court opinions as *fact* on Constitutional interpretation, rather than *opinion*. Law students are taught to analyze new issues within the framework constructed by 225 years of judicial interpretation.

So we begin at an extreme disadvantage because we instruct our future lawyers on 225 years of opinion as though there is no option but to accept this subsequent and extra-Constitutional commentary as sufficiently and rightly interpreting what the U.S. Constitution plainly says for itself. Granted, we must negotiate these opinions within our analysis of how we got to the current judicial view (and how to come back from this Constitutional boondoggle) because these opinions are of course viewed as binding legal precedent today.

However, to begin a proper analysis of correct Constitutional interpretation and build the proper framework from this foundation, we must, as Julie Andrews sang in *The Sound of Music*, start at the very beginning—a very good place to start.

This question of correct Constitutional interpretation is two-fold: First and more narrowly, how should government interpret and apply the actual text of the U.S. Constitution? By what standards and parameters and evidence of the Founding Fathers' intent should we understand the basic principles of government that are contained in the U.S. Constitution?

Second and more broadly, in what context should we read the U.S. Constitution? What standards and parameters and evidence of the universe as a whole delineate an objectively appropriate interpretation and application of the U.S. Constitution as the written law evidencing the Founders' intent for a specific form of human government?

Is there a universal standard for the role and limits of government we can appeal to? What about the problem of legislating morality?

A secular view of government teaches that objective morality is contained nowhere in appropriate Constitutional law and there is no universal standard or parameters for government, just that restraint which we impose on ourselves through the government's own action.

In this view, the standard of Constitutional interpretation changes with the pulse of the culture and, like a rubber band, can expand or contract based on the broadening or narrowing ideology structure of society. Not only is this structure of Constitutional interpretation consistently changing based on fluctuating morals of society, but is not actually morality at all—rather it is couched in terms of mere "reasonableness" for society with the goal simply to referee social relationships, not "impose" any fixed standard of absolute morality.

The root worldview of this ideology is secular humanism—that man is the sole originator of morality and capable of determining morality without existence of a God higher than man himself, and therefore morality becomes subjective to man's definition, interpretation, and application. The Council for Secular Humanism concisely states this premise of mere "reasonableness" in this declaration: "[B]ecause we are committed to secular public reasonableness, [we] would not express these ideas in moral terms that might discomfit others who share that commitment."[8]

An objective moral standard and fixed set of principles therefore poses a nagging problem.

In the secular humanist view, only that which can be empirically observed is true reality. Christopher Hitchens, perhaps the most notorious secular humanist, described this as a "naturalistic worldview" that "necessarily disbelieves in God"[9] and just as necessarily opposes "bad" ethical principles because of a "positive ethical outlook" that rejects any part of the universe that is metaphysical. The Council for Secular Humanism affirms an ethical system that is "rooted in the world of experience; objective; and equally accessible to every human who cares to inquire into the value issues."[10]

Quickly, we can see the conflict inherent in this worldview: a moral framework that attempts to be both "objective and equally accessible," purportedly able to make universal value judgments on moral right and wrong, yet that is also flexible and subjective, according to man's own individual value judgment and experience.

C.S. Lewis summed this problem, saying,

> "The very words *corrupt* and *degenerate* imply a doctrine of value and are therefore meaningless in this context. My point is that those who stand outside all judgments of value cannot have any ground for preferring one of their own impulses to another except the emotional strength of that impulse. We may legitimately hope that among the impulses which arise in the minds thus emptied of all 'rational' or 'spiritual' motives, some will be benevolent. I am very doubtful myself whether the benevolent impulses ... left to their merely natural strength and frequency as psychological events, will have much influence. I am very doubtful whether history shows us one example of a man who, having stepped outside traditional morality and attained power, has used that power benevolently. ... By the logic of their position they must just take their impulses as they come, from chance."[11]

Morality by definition cannot logically and *simultaneously* be:

1. Objective, universal, and equally accessible to every human; **and,**
2. Subjective, obliged to chance, and derived from man's own impulses.

Judeo-Christian theology teaches us the biblical theistic worldview of general revelation from God, which necessarily includes morality as a universal constant. General revelation (or "natural revelation") is a universal knowledge about reality and its existence from God, as to spiritual matters (metaphysical reality) and material matters (physical reality).

The biblical worldview also includes "special revelation"—or the specific ways that God has chosen to reveal Himself and Truth. This includes the Bible itself as the Word of God and the earthly ministry of Jesus Christ. For purposes of this book and a discussion of the origins of law and morality, we will focus on general revelation, but when we discuss the foundations of American law, we will see that the Founders referred to "the Laws of Nature and of Nature's God," which inherently encompass both general and special revelation.

As John Adams described in the quotation above, human understanding and awareness of our physical and metaphysical reality is this general revelation from our Maker, nature's God. Part of this general revelation is morality, given by God in our physical and metaphysical universe and contained in Scripture, and therefore as fundamental and non-negotiable as scientific fact.

Author and apologetics professor Nancy Pearcey described this fundamental "self-evident" knowledge of reality:

> "For example, no one really doubts that he or she exists (not in practice, at least). No one doubts that the material world is real (we all look both ways before crossing the street). Nor do we doubt our inner experiences like memories or pain. (If I say I have a headache, you don't ask, *How do you know?*) If anyone does deny these basic facts, we call him insane—or a philosopher. And even philosophers deny them only theoretically: [David] Hume himself said that, after

5

reasoning his way to radical skepticism in the solitude of his study, he would clear his mind by playing a good game of backgammon with his friends. [...]

The core claim of Common Sense realism was that these undeniable or self-evident truths of experience provide a firm foundation upon which to build the entire edifice of knowledge—like the foundation of a house. (By "common sense," [philosophers] did not mean practicality or horse sense, as we use the term today, but rather those truths known by universal human experience—*common* to all humanity.)

Most nineteenth-century thinkers included among the self-evident truths many of the basic teachings of Christianity, such as God's existence, His goodness, and His creation of the world. These were taken to be self-evident to reasonable people."[12]

Universal morality, a self-evident truth, is the central standard of right and wrong, including ethics in government action. And this is for our own good. As the Apostle Paul wrote, "All scripture is given by inspiration of God, and is profitable for doctrine, for reproof, for correction, for instruction in righteousness: That the man of God may be perfect, thoroughly furnished unto all good works."[13]

As we will discover, the text of the Declaration of Independence itself refers to these exact same "self-evident" truths, derived from general revelation.

The basic premise of a moral Constitutional interpretation comes from the reality that universal existence necessarily includes morality. The following chapters present the structured analysis of the legal concepts of legitimate authority, the scope and role of government, and the foundations of our Founding Documents (the Declaration of Independence and the U.S. Constitution) in this concept of fundamental, self-evident truths.

Intersection between "secular" government law and "sacred" moral law is *necessary* to any form of legitimate government and, as we will see, rooted firmly in foundation of America's revolutionary history at its very inception.

As Pearcey described in the Introduction to *Saving Leonardo* (the reader is encouraged to read this work in full):

> "A secular approach to politics first took root in the universities[.]… [S]cholars decided that the study of politics must be "scientific"—by which they meant value free. As a consequence, political theory was no longer animated by a moral vision. It became purely pragmatic. This represented a radical departure from the heritage of the American founders. At the birth of our nation, politics was assumed to be a profoundly moral enterprise—the pursuit of moral ideals such as justice, fairness, and the common good. James Madison, principal author of the U.S. Constitution, said the goal of government was to secure "the public good." … But today, after decades of treating politics as value free, many political scientists reject the very concept of a transcendent good. … Thus, the fact/value split—the idea that humans can have genuine knowledge only in the realm of empirical facts. Morality was reduced to subjective preferences. The term *values* means literally whatever the individual happens to value."[14]

This redefinition of objective values and morality itself gave way to a completely different meaning to government, its proper role, and the context and thus interpretation of the U.S. Constitution. Ironically, we fit the time and place in history with the plain meaning of any other historical document, including political commentary. We do not view Augustine's writings through a 21st Century lens, nor do we consider any of the Greek philosophers' political historical documents to be "fluid"—that is, changing their meaning according to whatever new meaning we desire to give.

Why is the U.S. Constitution literally the *only* document through the course of human history that is so magical that it can change its own meaning via shifting political winds?

Because the secular humanists are selling a legal fiction. The U.S. Constitution is no such "magical" document. To understand the very plain meaning of the U.S. Constitution and how it has been subsequently transformed, we must go back in history and view the U.S. Constitution through the lens of the Founders as its authors— and start at the very beginning.

CHAPTER 2

THE FOUNDERS AND THEIR RELATIONSHIP TO THE LAW

"The practice of morality being necessary for the well being of society, He [God] has taken care to impress its precepts so indelibly on our hearts that they shall not be effaced by the subtleties of our brain. We all agree in the obligation of the moral principles of Jesus and nowhere will they be found delivered in greater purity than in His discourses."[15]

- Thomas Jefferson

The debate rages on within Christian and secular communities regarding the Founding Fathers and their faith. Were they Christians or Deists or Atheists or something else? If they were Christian, did they have a correct Biblical worldview?

Does this debate matter to American Constitutional Law and our interpretation of the law today?

Some authors and historians argue that because there is evidence the Founders referred to biblical truths in personal letters and historical documents such as the Federalist Papers and because many led outwardly faith-based lives, attended church, and prayed to God, we can *on that basis* infer that the categorical intent of the Founders in the formation of American government was equally Christianly principled, or at the very least, heavily biblically influenced.

It is certainly true many of the Founding Fathers quoted from the Bible, discussed biblical principles related to government, and held out their faith as influencing the rationale of their political ideology.

For example, James Madison, principal author of the Federalist Papers, principal drafter of the U.S. Constitution, and fourth President of the United States, wrote,

> "I have sometimes thought there could be no stronger testimony in favor of Religion or against temporal Enjoyments even the most rational and manly than for men who occupy the most honorable and gainful departments and are rising in reputation and wealth, publicly to declare their unsatisfactoriness by becoming fervent Advocates in the cause of Christ, and I wish you may give in your Evidence in this way. Such instances have seldom occurred, therefore they would be more striking and would be instead of a 'Cloud of Witnesses.'"[16]

John Adams, drafter and signatory of the Declaration of Independence and second President of the United States, wrote,

> "The general principles on which the fathers achieved independence were the general principles of Christianity. I will avow that I then believed, and now believe, that those general principles of Christianity are as eternal an immutable as the existence and attributes of God."[17]

George Washington, signatory of the U.S. Constitution and first President of the United States, wrote,

"Whereas it is the duty of all Nations to acknowledge the providence of Almighty God, to obey his will, to be grateful for his benefits, and humbly to implore his protection and favor"[18] and, "Reason and experience both forbid us to expect that national morality can prevail in exclusion of religious principle."[19]

Benjamin Rush, signatory of the Declaration of Independence and attendee of the Continental Congress, said,

"I do not believe that the Constitution was an offspring of inspiration, but I am as satisfied that it is as much the work of a Divine Providence as any of the miracles recorded in the Old and New Testament."[20]

The examples and quotations are numerous.

There is indeed ample evidence to suggest and even conclude that the Founders were biblically-based Christians and embraced the Judeo-Christian worldview, which extended into their politics. But there are also scholars who suggest there is evidence arguing that some of the Founders, such as Jefferson and Franklin, were no more than Enlightenment Christians (as opposed to what we today would consider Evangelical Christians) or merely Deists.[21]

But is this debate ultimately dispositive for correct Constitutional interpretation? The argument that "the Founders were Christians, so therefore we must interpret the U.S. Constitution based on Christian principles" is not necessarily persuasive or conclusive when applied to the issue of Constitutional interpretation and demands for biblically-based opinions on laws today.

Is this really the *best* argument and basis for a moral U.S. Constitution? No. "Constitutional intent"—the philosophical argument of interpreting the text of the U.S. Constitution based on what we can deduce the Founders wanted, meant, or intended—does not necessarily end with the Founder's personal belief system.

Extrapolation from the beliefs of many of the Founders may be a valid historical argument for an Evangelical Christian "stamp" on most of the Founders and a partially persuasive argument for biblically-based Constitutional interpretation, but importantly, it is not entirely legally conclusive, and therefore, probably not the best basis from which to assert biblical morality within the legal Constitutional interpretation debate.

We are not seeking to resign morality to the realm of passé American history. We are still actively arguing the validity of an objective biblical moral worldview interpretation for the U.S. Constitution today. Therefore, we need a *legal* basis.

Beyond preventing further relegation of the Founders' faith to a mere "historical record," the primary reason we need a legal basis is because of the counter-argument to the profession of the Founders' faith as a nexus to Constitutional interpretation: Simply because the majority of Founders embraced a particular faith in their personal lives, and even if we could prove conclusively that they were evangelical Christians, *that* alone does not categorically require future legislative and judicial bodies to interpret American laws and social governance from the same "personal" views.

For example, we may have two Congressional senators who equally profess a Christian faith, but one embraces Democratic political ideals and the other a Republican viewpoint, so when it comes to voting on specific legislative bills, their political affiliations may influence and even override their personal professions of faith. While we may take issue with that outcome for other very appropriate reasons, we can see it is logically not enough to conclude that one's personal profession of faith necessarily predicts his or her political values, actions, or intent.

But even more importantly, the personal viewpoint or political affiliation of a legislator has no relevance when an issue of interpretation arises. The judiciary looks primarily at the *text* of the statute or law to determine its meaning. Occasionally, when a law is vague or over-broad, the courts will also look to the legislative history of the law—the minutes recorded in the legislative session when the legislators debated the language and settled on the final version—to attempt to understand what the legislators intended. Personal ideology or even personal identity of the legislative body is almost entirely irrelevant.

Therefore, we need an objective, not "personal," standard of law. This is even more imperative because we are dealing with today's cultural definition of values being personal and entirely subjective, with fact/knowledge claims separate from moral/value claims.

And of course, the secular counterpoint to the Founders' faith argument is rooted in what has become the political and philosophical notion of "separation of church and state" (a Jeffersonian phrase taken entirely out of context, as we will see). This phrase does not appear anywhere in the U.S. Constitution or in the other Founding Documents, including the Declaration of Independence and the Federalist Papers.[22]

Instead, we see the structure of the American form of government as specifically excluding government power to establish a national religion (akin to a theocracy), yet simultaneously protecting the individual freedom to exercise religion according to sincerely held faith and beliefs, in the text of the First Amendment, and we also see that the Founders exercised and cited specific objective moral law in establishing the new union. This is not a "separation of church and state" in the sense that secularists use this phrase now—arguing that any moral and religious beliefs and government must be mutually exclusive.

So where did this notion of total "separation of church and state" and a completely amoral, religiously sterile interpretation of the U.S. Constitution originate that still somehow simultaneously protects and preserves free exercise of religion and sincerely held beliefs?

To sort through that seeming dichotomy, understand what the First Amendment is actually saying, perceive the actual basis of authority upon which the Founders predicated our system of government, and from where those rights were legitimately derived, we have look at evidence beyond the personal faith and sincerely held religious beliefs of the Founders to the actual text of the Founding Documents themselves.

Simply because an argument exists that the Founders' original intent may have been from a personal perspective of biblical principles, this reasoning does not necessarily establish that such "legislative history" (i.e., the evidence of the Founders' personal faith) cannot be overridden in the context of judicial opinion.

While the Founders' personal faith and political beliefs do matter, just as intent matters to any legislative history, it is perhaps not a *sufficient* argument for Constitutional interpretation based on biblical principles when engaging a secular thinker in this conversation. In this sense, though we know a great deal about who the Founders were personally, we must first look to the text of the Founding Documents and also to the legislative history. We also must look at the Founders capacity as legislators—who they were professionally.

Importantly, while this debate should be quite clear from the evidence that we will discuss in the subsequent chapters, those who espouse the secular agenda have attempted to muddy the waters even more by inserting into the mainstream populace the notion that the judicial branch can *create law* through its opinions.

This is completely and utterly false.

The secular agenda asserts that even if we know absolutely the particular intent of a legislature for a particular law, that law can still be overturned, undermined, or reinterpreted based on other reasons that the reviewers (usually the Judiciary) believe are more important.

We have seen many examples of this in Supreme Court opinions, most notably recently in *Obergefell* where many states purposefully had laws establishing protection of traditional heterosexual marriage, yet the Court decided to override the states' clearly legislated intent in favor of valuing "marriage equality," or the idea that same-sex couples had a fundamental "right" to state-recognized marriage. [23]

A Constitutional Law lecture at The University of California Hastings College of the Law bluntly summed up this legal farce: "[A]ll political actors know that the U.S. Supreme Court often operates as a super-legislature, and thus that the moral and political views of the Justices are decisive criteria for their appointment. This almost banal truth is, however, rarely discussed in the public confirmation process, but it is common knowledge among political and legal insiders."[24]

So we see that even if we have a very clear legislative history and record exists as to how the lawgivers formed the language for a specific statute and why, that record does not automatically guarantee that the statute itself will not be overridden as (arguably) unconstitutional, unfair, too vague, or too broad, or simply that we as a society now value one freedom more than another, by a "scrutinizing" (read: politically active) judicial court.

This argument is why the secular community reasons that the concept and doctrine of *judicial review* overrides any speculation or even any actually known intent of the Founders, and why the U.S. Constitution itself should be considered a "fluid" document—subject to the whim of the current majority social viewpoint, as expressed through the majority of five lawyers on the Supreme Court.

But this is a failing argument that is premised in a flagrantly unconstitutional view of the Supreme Court as a super-legislative body legally capable of enacting law.

Justice Antonin Scalia wrote in his dissent in *Obergefell*,

> "I write separately to call attention to this Court's threat to American democracy. … The substance of today's decree is not of immense personal importance to me … It is of overwhelming importance, however, who it is that rules me. Today's decress says that my Ruler, and the Ruler of 320 million Americans coast-to-coast, is a majority of the nine lawyers on the Supreme Court."[25]

Judicial review itself is the doctrine and process by which legislative and executive actions are literally reviewed by the Judiciary. Notably, this doctrine was not specified within the text of the U.S. Constitution itself, though the theory and design schematic of separation of powers between the branches was forefront during the Constitutional Convention. Rather, the doctrine was given its tangible power through the first act of judicial review by the U.S. Supreme Court in 1803 in a landmark case, *Marbury v. Madison*.[26]

Marbury was the first case that the Supreme Court had to resolve that asked the questions: What is Congress's power in relation to the U.S. Constitution and what is the Supreme Court's role and authority to oversee Congressional action (and, by extension, the states' legislative action)?

Article III of the U.S. Constitution establishes the judiciary and provides its authority and scope: "The judicial power of the United States shall be vested in one Supreme Court, and in such inferior courts as the Congress may from time to time ordain and establish."[27] The text continues, "The judicial power shall extend to all cases, in law and equity, arising under this Constitution, the laws of the United States, and treaties made, or which shall be made, under their authority[.]"[28]

As one author concisely and accurately states about this Constitutional text, "Unlike legislatures, which create law, and the executive branch, which is charged with faithfully executing the law, the judicial power is one of rendering judgment about law's bearing on specific cases."[29]

The Supreme Court in *Marbury*, under the leadership of Chief Justice John Marshall, determined that it is the proper role of the Judiciary to interpret what the U.S. Constitution permits and what it prohibits within the specific contexts of cases. Because Congress cannot pass laws that are contrary to the U.S. Constitution, the Judiciary (ultimately through the Supreme Court) acts as the safeguard to compare the legislative acts against the U.S. Constitution as Supreme Law and decide if those laws are in conformance or if they should be struck down as "unconstitutional."

Judicial review in this capacity was never challenged by the other two branches of government, and has been the foundational threshold for the Judiciary to increasingly become the most powerful branch of government. While the principle and legal theory of judicial review itself is arguably derived from correct authority and is not in itself problematic, it has become increasingly misapplied by a culture of activists. Once the Supreme Court subsequently extended its review to make its opinion binding precedent on *everyone* (not just the parties to the case), they in effect became higher than the U.S. Constitution itself. This is wrongful and unconstitutional.

The entire intent of the U.S. Constitution was a balance of powers among the federal government's branches, and to specifically *limit* the federal government's authority with respect to the states—a principle commonly called "federalism."

Federalism is the political concept that provides for the U.S. Constitution continuing to operate as the supreme law of the land, even over and above the states' authority to legislate in some matters. The Supreme Court also gave itself power through *Marbury* to review state government action and determine if a state is errantly establishing law that usurps legitimate federal government authority.

Importantly, the Tenth Amendment (the last amendment included in the original Bill of Rights) explicitly states that all powers not specifically granted through the text of the U.S. Constitution shall be reserved to the states.[30] However, this principle does not operate within the context of the U.S. Constitution to infer that the states then have the power to legislate contrary to the U.S. Constitution, which is the Supreme Law of the land, or outside the scope of legitimate governmental action.

Federalism allows the Supreme Court to review some laws of the states and keep them accountable, but *only* reviewing power to the extent that the federal judiciary has jurisdiction—the legal authority over certain cases or laws. As we will see in later chapters, the tension of how to apply federalism appropriately and legally has become extremely one-sided in favor of a stronger federal government, and this idea of federal judicial oversight of the states is one of the primary mechanisms employed by the Supreme Court to usurp more and more of the states' rightful legislative authority and ultimately, the rights of individuals.

Although the text of the U.S. Constitution and Alexander Hamilton's famous statement in Federalist 78[31] tell us that the judicial branch was conceptualized as the weakest of the three branches of government because of its inability to create law or enact the law, the introduction and precedent of judicial review swiftly gave immeasurable power to the highest judicial body—the U.S. Supreme Court—to be the last word and therefore final decision on laws' interpretations, application, and constitutionality.

The collateral consequence of implementing the doctrine of judicial review is that there is virtually no accountability within the judiciary itself or within the other branches of government, legislative or executive, on the U.S. Supreme Court as the highest source of review.

As Justice Robert H. Jackson wisely observed about the U.S. Supreme Court while he was a sitting justice, "Reversal by a higher court is not proof that justice is thereby better done. There is no doubt that if there were a super-Supreme Court, a substantial proportion of our reversals of state courts would also be reversed. We are not final because we are infallible, but we are infallible only because we are final."[32]

The power of judicial review has become a nearly absolute power when there is no review or check or balance upon the highest source of review—especially for the states. The U.S. Supreme Court is well titled as the "Court of last resort," and the "highest Court in the land," among other nicknames.

Returning then to our initial observation, while the Founders' personal faith is of historical significance and even some relevance to the constitutional interpretation argument, we see that we cannot decisively win the debate based solely on the premise that the Founders' personal faith must dictate a biblically-based moral U.S. Constitution when the doctrine of judicial review is now governing the entirety of government itself.

Does that mean then that the law, and specifically the U.S. Constitution as the highest law, is indeed subject to review and the whim of reinterpretation by generations of newly comprised sitting U.S. Supreme Courts? Not at all. The U.S. Constitution itself must still *mean* something definitive and objectively concrete to be meaningful, understood, and then upheld as the highest law of the land.

Remember, the *Marbury* Court held that it is the role of the Judiciary to interpret what the U.S. Constitution does and does not permit, which necessarily presumes that the U.S. Constitution says and means something that can be objectively determined. This objective determination can be properly deduced from the legal basis of authority upon which the U.S. Constitution is predicated.

As we will see as we unpack this legal basis, for a law or set of laws like the U.S. Constitution to have any validity, it must have a source of legitimate authority. That source of authority is the foundation of the law, and the objective meaning of the law must be in conformance to its authority.

For example, the U.S. Supreme Court, though currently immeasurably powerful, still does not in fact possess the authority to override or alter the U.S. Constitution, but must act *in accordance* with it, because the Court derives its authority from the U.S. Constitution. Nor does the Supreme Court have actual authority to enact law.

Returning again to the text in Article III, "The judicial power shall extend to all cases, in law and equity, *arising **under** this Constitution,* the laws of the United States, and treaties made, or which shall be made, **under** *their authority*"[33] (emphasis added).

The judiciary as a whole and specifically the U.S. Supreme Court only possesses authority **under** the U.S. Constitution and within the scope and limited boundaries that the U.S. Constitution itself ordained and established and still regulates as the Supreme Law of the land.

So then, the U.S. Constitution itself is one of the sole remaining "checks" on the Judiciary. While the concept of judicial review is consistent with the Constitutional requirement for "one Supreme Court," judicial review can only extend to courts and cases *below* the U.S. Constitution and safeguarded by the "ceiling" of the Supreme Court—not upward and into reframing and reinterpreting the U.S. Constitution itself.

Since the U.S. Constitution is a written document that must mean something objectively determinable, we must understand by what basis we deduce the correct meaning and from where the U.S. Constitution derives its authority.

The most critical and foundational aspect in determining and understanding the meaning, intent, and authoritative basis for the rightful and objectively correct interpretation of the U.S. Constitution necessarily begins with the fact that nearly all of the most prominent and influential Founders were *lawyers*.

Consider:

- The two principal drafters of the Declaration of Independence, Thomas Jefferson and John Adams, were lawyers.
- The five members of the Declaration Committee (Jefferson, Adams, Franklin, Sherman, and Livingston) were all lawyers.
- Of the 56 signers of the Declaration of Independence, 25 were lawyers.
- Of the 55 framers of the U.S. Constitution, 32 were lawyers.

A sampling of the professional portraits of the most influential Founders include:

Thomas Jefferson

- – William & Mary College
- – Admitted to the Virginia Bar
- – Principal author of the Declaration of Independence
- – Drafter of the U.S. Constitution

John Adams

- Harvard
- Admitted to the Massachusetts Bar
- Assisted Jefferson in drafting the Declaration of Independence
- One of the five members of the Declaration Committee

Benjamin Franklin

- Universities of Edinburgh & Oxford
- Honorary Doctor of Laws (educated as a lawyer but never practiced)
- One of the five members of the Declaration Committee
- Signed the U.S. Constitution

Alexander Hamilton

- King's College (Columbia University)
- Admitted to the New York Bar
- Principal drafter of the U.S. Constitution
- Principal author of the Federalist Papers

John Jay

- King's College (Columbia University)
- Admitted to the New York Bar
- Principal author of the Federalist Papers
- First Supreme Court Chief Justice

James Madison

- Princeton University
- Studied law for public policy (educated as a lawyer but never practiced)
- Principal author of the Federalist Papers
- Principal drafter of the U.S. Constitution

Roger Sherman

- Admitted to the Connecticut Bar
- Member of the Declaration Committee
- Only Founder to sign the Declaration of Independence, Articles of Association, Articles of Confederation, and the U.S. Constitution

Robert Livingston

- King's College (Columbia University)
- Admitted to the New York Bar
- Member of the Declaration Committee
- Chancellor of New York and administered the oath of office to President George Washington

John Marshall

- College of William and Mary
- Admitted to the Virginia Bar
- Fourth Chief Justice of the Supreme Court
- Signatory of the U.S. Constitution

The Declaration Committee

- Composed of five lawyers: Jefferson, Adams, Franklin, Sherman, and Livingston
- Principal drafters: Jefferson and Adams

The most important fact to Constitutional Law and its correct, objective interpretation is not whether the Founders were Christians and exercised discernable faith, but the fact that the Founders were lawyers. This is the key fact to determining the legal basis and source of authority for the U.S. Constitution.

As we will see, lawyers have a particular and distinct philosophy, assignment of meaning, and understanding of the law and legal documents. Legal documents presume that the philosophies, rules, and legal meaning of the law are applied by the lawyer author and understood by the lawyer reader.

Litigation of a particular legal document, such as a contract, does not require that the drafter or the parties to the agreement are present to tell the court what they intended and how to understand what they wrote. The meaning can be understood or implied from the text of the document itself because it is a legal document. Good attorneys know how to tell future reviewers their intent and authority through the document itself.

A valid legal document will contain several key things (among others, depending on what type of document it is):

First, lawyers will cite the authority by which the document effects the legal change that it intends, and thus why it is a legal document rather than any other non-legal document. This cited authority can be a statute or rule, a theory of law, or simply that the parties are entering an agreement by their own authority under civil law.

Second, this authority must be *legitimate*. We will discuss the concept of legitimacy further in later chapters, but the essence of this idea is that a document cannot be a valid legal document if the authority cited is not an actual or appropriate authority and is therefore not legitimate. If a lawyer cited a rule that was outdated or had been overruled as my authority, the judge would tell her that her authority was not legitimate and the basis on which she founded her argument upon was invalid.

Third, even a legitimate authority must also be correctly applied in a specific instance. This is called the *rationale*. For example, it would be irrational to cite a rule about speeding limits as a defense to not registering one's car properly. Speeding limits are a different rule and, although a legitimate authority in instances where the issue is going 65 in a 55 MPH zone, bear no rational relationship to a situation of failure to register one's car. So attempting to apply this rule is irrational—it has no legitimate authority in context. Both of these rules involve the car, but each applies in different contexts and is legitimate authority under a different legal basis and in different instances.

Importantly, sometimes lawyers will disagree on the rationale and why a particular legitimate authority does or does not apply to a specific instance. An inherent part of judicial review includes a legal determination whether a specific citation of authority is correctly and appropriately applied. This is generally the rationale of the court's opinion. The law in this sense is sometimes debatable, but there can be and are still objective and determinable *meaning* to law. When a law as applied to a specific instance is debatable, the court then must refer back to the higher authority.

Much of the confusion about Constitutional Law interpretation centers around the question of where to go in the chain of authority when the language of the U.S. Constitution, intent, or application is debatable. If the U.S. Constitution is the supreme law of the land, what happens when there is a disagreement in judicial review about the U.S. Constitution itself?

The answer to this question necessarily depends on the source of the U.S. Constitution's authority.

The Founders as lawyers knew this, objectively providing the answer in clear terms that other lawyers understand. Lawyers will provide the authority, legitimacy, and rationale in specific words and phrases that other lawyers understand without having to speak directly to each other. Lawyers will often say, "The legal document speaks for itself." This is what they mean.

If you have ever read a contract for sale of real estate or the "Terms and Conditions of Use" for a smartphone or tablet, you will readily understand there is a distinct legal language and particular meaning that lawyers give to words and phrases, not to complicate a sentence structure into intelligible "legalese," but to be so precise in legal terms that other lawyers can understand their intent through this mutually understood objective meaning. Lawyers call these words and phrases "terms of art."

For example, the term "consideration" in a legal contract has a far different meaning than in general conversational English. Consider the difference in the following two sentences:

Conversational English Language:

"I will give your opinion due consideration when making my decision."

English Legal Language:

"In consideration of the purchase of the used car, Buyer shall pay Seller $500."

In normal conversational language, we use the term "consideration" to mean deliberation, contemplation, or reflective thought. But in legal language, lawyers use the term "consideration" to mean "something of value" or "a bargained-for exchange." The legal language specifically does not mean, "In contemplation or deliberation of the purchase of the used car." but rather, "This is the quantifiably valuable and legal exchange: a used car for $500."

Consideration in the legal context is a noun and a thing, and for any contract to be legal and enforceable, "consideration" the *thing* must be present. This meaning is far different from the normative usage in regular English conversation. So then, the meaning dramatically changes when this same word converts from a regularly understood

English language word to a legal term of art that has a specific and particularly distinct meaning to lawyers.

We know that legal terms are used in legal documents. When a document is legal and drafted by a lawyer, we know that the words and phrases have the understood legal meaning, rather than the conversational English meaning.

Now reading a written contract, we understand why the language appears to be confusing, nonsensical, and sometimes even counterintuitive, *unless* you are a lawyer and understand the legal "terms of art" and their particular, contextual meaning. Lawyers make sense of legal documents because they understand this particular, objective meaning.

This and other distinctions in legal practice become incredibly important when we look at the Founding Documents, including the Declaration of Independence and the U.S. Constitution. These documents are not just historically significant documents, but utterly more importantly, *legal* documents. The terms of art, legal language, legal philosophy, and legal power that the Founders as lawyers understood are inherently and critically important to correctly interpreting what these legal documents objectively say and mean.

In a legal sense, these Founding Documents do speak for themselves. We can know their intent by understanding their legal authority, legitimacy, and rationale. The U.S. Supreme Court (and any other court) is not free to depart from the legal authority and plain meaning of the U.S. Constitution, but is **under** its authority. As Article III states, the Supreme Court is bound by the U.S. Constitution's law as a controlling legal document.

The U.S. Constitution's establishment of the Judiciary created a commitment to the "rule of law"—the legal term of art meaning a "rule of *rules*, rather than the rule of *rulers*." The Founding Documents, among other things, created a universe of rules to which American government would be subject, which is specifically not a set of rulers who may change the supreme law at whim, and certainly not the rule of a life-tenured, non–elected Supreme Court. The Supreme Court only has its authority and legitimacy **under** the U.S. Constitution.

The U.S. Constitution, likewise, is not free to depart from its legal authority, and any interpretation in contradiction to its authority is necessarily invalid. Answering this question of Constitutional authority therefore becomes central to objectively determining Constitutional interpretation.

Thus, we know that the Founding Documents (specifically, the Declaration of Independence and the U.S. Constitution) are legal documents because of their context, language, rationale, and use, effect, and legal authority. These documents were more than philosophical declarations—they affected the United States legally.

These documents established a legal separation from England, constituted a legally recognized sovereign nation, established a legal government, and delivered the legal basis in legitimate authority for the U.S. Constitution as Supreme Law of the land. Just as a deed of sale for real estate must necessarily have the legal authority to transfer property ownership, or a criminal law statute must necessarily have the legal authority to impose punitive sanctions, so the Founding Documents must also have legal authority and legal effect to be considered legal documents.

Legal documents must also contain certain terms in order to be effective. Using the deed of sale example, that document must, among other things, define the geographical area of physical land being sold, identify the seller (current owner) and buyer (new owner), and specify other legally necessary aspects of the transfer of real estate ownership, and comply with all other legal requirements to have the actual effect of transferring legal title ownership from the seller to the buyer.

Underpinning the plain terms or the "nuts and bolts" of this legal document is the authority by which the sale takes place—the owner's legitimate title to the property; the seller's legitimate buying power; the legitimate legal basis for the transaction. If these necessary legal terms are not set out, the document generally becomes void for lack of authority, and generates no actual legal effect.

For example, compare the legal effect of a marriage license to a love letter. Both are written documents and may involve the same people and the same demonstration of their affection for each other and loving intent, but one clearly is a legal document and the other clearly is not. Compare then the actual legal effect of the Declaration of Independence or U.S. Constitution with the mere historical opinion of a contemporaneous document such as Thomas Paine's *Common Sense*.[34]

If the Declaration of Independence or U.S. Constitution had no actual legal authority or effect, they would have been simply more historical musings and philosophical works by authors who sought to comment on the political events of the day. The Declaration of Independence and the U.S. Constitution would have generated no actual legal effect. But certainly, the Founding Documents are legal documents.

We will look at the legal context, legal language, and legal effect of the Founding Documents more closely, but first we will discuss the law itself. The next step to understanding the legal basis and meaning of the Founding Documents is to have a clear understanding of the concept of legitimacy in law and what philosophies underpin the Founding Documents, as understood by the Founders qua *lawyers*.

Understanding how lawyers define the law itself is centrally important to correctly interpreting the meaning of the Founding Documents, which in turn is critically important to answering the question of where the U.S. Constitution derives its authority.

CHAPTER 3

UNDERSTANDING THE LAW AND ITS AUTHORITY AND LEGITIMACY

"It is the duty of all to acknowledge that the Divine Law which requires us to love God with all our heart and our neighbor as ourselves, on pain of eternal damnation, is Holy, just, and good. ... The revealed law of God is the rule of our duty."[35]

- *Roger Sherman*

What do we mean when we say "the law?" There are several correct responses to this question, depending on the context of our response.

First, the law is a **philosophical construct**, and the concept of jurisprudence is the study and theory of law. American jurisprudence is the study and focus of American history and its law. Within jurisprudence as a whole, lawyers are philosophers and debate what the law means, what the law values, and what the law should be.

The philosophy of the law can be heavily influenced by any number of sources, well beyond the boundaries of American jurisprudence, our government, and the last 225 years of American history. Philosophy of the law does not in and of itself have any practical effect—it is entirely theoretical. We might very enthusiastically debate any number of hypothetical situations, such as what the law should be for a space-age community on Mars, but these debates ultimately are exercises in academic theory.

Second, the law is also a ***statutory construct***, and government statutes, case law, legal documents, and judicial opinions are what lawyers call "blackletter" law—the written text of the law and written interpretation and application of that text, which define what members of a society must do and must not do or what individual parties have agreed to do or not do. These laws are derived largely from human design (usually legislators, but also private parties in contracts between themselves) and can vary from society to society, state to state, country to country, and contract to contract.

Blackletter law can be influenced by diverse philosophical doctrines, but generally American law operates under a legal doctrine called *stare decisis*, which is the rule that a previous law or judicial opinion of a higher court is binding on a lower court and, regardless of the lower court's personal opinion about the precedent, the precedent must be followed. The lower court does not have the authority to overturn a higher court's ruling.

For example, a federal court of appeals does not have the authority to go against or disregard a ruling on the same issue from the U.S. Supreme Court. The practical effect of this rule is that even though a federal appellate judge may have a philosophical disagreement with the U.S. Supreme Court, he or she cannot overrule or reverse the U.S. Supreme Court. (We see this is consistent with Article III of the U.S. Constitution's establishment of "one Supreme Court."[36]) The "binding precedent" means that the lower court is bound by the law of the higher court.

However, not all "higher" courts are binding on *all* lower courts. While the Colorado Supreme Court is a higher court than the California Court of Appeals, it is only a higher court within its own state. Colorado's state Supreme Court does not have jurisdiction over California's state courts, so California's court is not bound by a Colorado Supreme Court decision. It may choose to follow a Colorado opinion because it finds that opinion persuasive, but it is not required to do so.

This is a very important distinction when we discuss the proper role of the U.S. Supreme Court and its jurisdiction in state issues, such as in *Obergefell*. The idea that the Supreme Court can reach and decide the law on any and all issues it selects is the primary reason that the doctrine of judicial review has had the practical effect of making the U.S. Supreme Court actually supreme—a super-legislative body and without a practical governmental mechanism of oversight.

Third and finally, the law is also a ***scientific construct***, and so-called "laws of nature" are defined by the empirical world around us and are discovered by us. No human government, past or present, invented the law of gravity—we merely discovered it (i.e. figured out that it existed), labeled it, and sought to understand how and when it works and is applied.

While humans can sometimes manipulate the laws of nature in various contexts—we learned how to fly airplanes in spite of gravity—humans are not the legislators of nature's laws. Rather, we are forced to be subject to nature's laws *unless* they can be and are manipulated. Humans cannot debate or negotiate the law of gravity. It exists independent of government authority and judicial review, whether or not we choose to believe in it, whether or not we can manipulate it, and regardless of whether or not we want it to exist.

The law in this sense is above and outside any human government or legislative body and binds man to its higher authority, regardless of our objections, our beliefs, or even our understanding of the law.

The law then, as a whole, is comprised of two segments: First, laws that are clearly defined, discoverable, and unchangeable, and second, laws that are debatable, man-made, and sometimes subject to change. When the law is "rigid" (unchangeable) and when it is "fluid" (changeable) depends on the law in question and occasionally the context.

As Frederic Bastiat observed, "Life, liberty, and property do not exist because men have made laws. On the contrary, it was the fact that life, liberty, and property existed beforehand that caused men to make laws in the first place."[37]

Importantly, the law, defined as including the philosophical, statutory, *and* scientific constructs of law, also inherently includes moral law. Where does moral law fit within the three identified constructs of law and what are its origins? Man or something outside man?

Secular humanist and progressive theorists argue that morality is purely a social construct and therefore whatever moral law exists is exclusively within the realm of the statutory construct. The Council for Secular Humanism states, "We are opposed to absolutist [objective] morality, yet we maintain that objective standards emerge, and ethical values and principles may be discovered in the course of ethical deliberation."[38]

Secular humanist philosopher Theodore Schick, Jr. writes,

> "Fundamentalists correctly perceive that universal moral standards are required for the proper functioning of society. But they erroneously believe that God is the only possible source of such standards. ...[I]t is possible to have a universal morality without God [originating in man]. Contrary to what the fundamentalists would have us believe, then, what our society really needs is not more religion but a richer notion of the nature of morality."[39]

This argument assumes then that all morality is subject to man's approval and derived from man and his government, while simultaneously asserting that it is still possible to have universal morality. But how can the conceded "nature of morality" possibly be universal if derived from man? This is a self-defeating claim. A universal law is by definition derived from a source other than man, such as physical and metaphysical reality or God.

Philosopher and apologist Francis Schaeffer said,

> "We must understand what we are talking about when we use the word Humanism. Humanism means that *the man is the measure of all things.* If this other final reality of material or energy shaped by pure chance is the final reality, it gives no meaning to life. It gives no value system. It gives no basis for law, and therefore, in this case, man must be the measure of all things. ... If indeed the final reality is silent about these values, then man must generate them from himself. ... Specifically, in this view, there is no place for any knowledge from God."[40]

Natural law theorists and theistic apologists (including Schaeffer) argue that moral law is part of the scientific construct—that is moral law is discoverable, objective, and applicable to all of mankind throughout history and in this sense exactly like empirical scientific laws. Moral law exists whether or not governments agree with it because moral law is outside of man's ability to manipulate or negotiate.

Schaeffer observed, "[L]aw is king, law is above the lawmakers, and God is above the law... And this is a part of true spirituality."[41] Moral law therefore *must* have a higher origin than man, precisely for the same reason the laws of science are not derived from man: morality is universal.

Part of this argument presumes that government has the ability to legislate *in accordance* with universal moral laws (like it does in accordance with empirical scientific laws), so there is naturally some overlap into the statutory construct, but the primary distinction is that moral law is derived from discoverable nature (theists would go further and say derived from God), but specifically not from man or his government.

Readily recognizable in legislative debates is the idea of "legislating morality." That is, creating statutes that contain an element, basis, or rationale of a moral law principle.

For example, respecting the pro-life/abortion issue and determining the government's laws on this issue, much of the debate focuses on the morality of life and the value to society in either demanding preservation of that life or allowing the mother to choose to keep or extinguish that life. Because the argument framed as "life" presumes that there *is* a life, theists have argued the moral component that life inherently has value and we have no ability as a government to legislate against the laws of nature, including morality.

In response, secular humanist theorists have then attempted to redefine life and personhood in an endeavor to reconcile the conflict between the value of preserving life and the supposed value of freedom to choose to extinguish that life. If there is no "life" (defined as human or "viable personhood") and the argument is not inherently a moral one, then we can see how the framework becomes more easily confined to the statutory construct.

But the pro-choice argument and any other argument premised against "legislating morality" still necessarily depends on the assumption that moral law is not part of the scientific construct and therefore human government is free to debate morality as only a social statutory construct and we are thereby free to choose how and when to legislate it.

While it is true that man can legislate morality to the extent that we can impose human enforcement and consequences for breaching morally based statutes, this narrow scope of moral law does not provide for morality that is outside of human authority and exists like scientific laws—whether or not we choose to acknowledge it exists.

And as we have already seen, the law is, and always has been, used to impose a specific worldview on culture. The law contains a set of principles for government of a well-regulated society. We therefore cannot escape the fact that law is *always* inherently moral.

In a diagram, moral law is above statutory law in authority and therefore encompasses statutory law. It looks like this:

Fig. 1

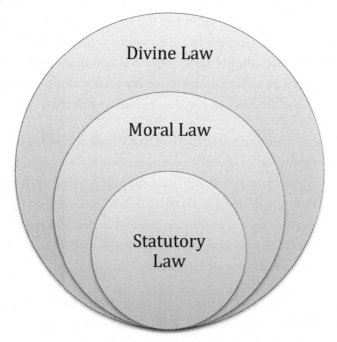

Venn Diagram of Circles with Moral
Law containing Statutory Law

But lawyers, politicians, and philosophers throughout history have sought to separate scientific laws from moral ones, and current American culture is even attempting to remove moral law from the statutory construct. So-called "moral debates" are now largely confined to the realm of the philosophical construct, and secular culture continues to specifically exclude morality from nature's laws and science and thus provide an apparent basis to also exclude morality from statutory laws under the thin guise of "personal freedom"—the idea that if morality is not universal in nature, the government should not legislate it either.

The diagram has progressed and now looks like this:

Fig. 2

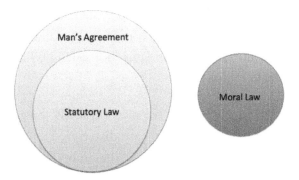

Venn Diagram of Circles with Moral Law outside Statutory Law

Scientific facts are called "laws of science" while moral facts are creatively renamed "moral principles," implying that the moral in question is not an absolute and is not objectively concrete in the same way a law of science is. We are taught that we can make up principles in the same way we might create a proverb or saying, and it might be good advice, but we can take it or leave it at our own discretion or amend it at will.

The secular argument continues, because we are supposedly free from objective, forced moral influence, we therefore should not impose our own *philosophical* morality on others, especially through government legislation and the statutory construct of law.

What about the scientific construct?

Morality then has no acknowledgement within or practical effect in the scientific construct or the statutory construct. Once we take morality out of the objective scientific construct, the logical end of that argument resigns morality to merely philosophical unless legislated by man's government, upon man's accord, and freely debatable and changeable to moral compass of the majority's will.

Proponents of this demotion of moral law also offer the argument that nature and science is inherently amoral (without moral influence). One author attributed a completely impersonal, mechanical autonomy to scientific laws, saying, "Nature is morally blind, without values. It churns along, following its own laws, not caring who or what gets in its way."[42]

This concept of nature and science expressly omits any moral influence. Whereas scientific laws are discovered or "found" in the universe, secular philosophers argue that moral law is "made" or constructed and entirely dependent on human ratification.

Schaeffer wrote, "Secular humanism means that the man is the measure of all things… But it is not only that man must start from himself in the area of knowledge and learning, but any value system must come arbitrarily from man himself by arbitrary choice."[43]

This tension over where moral law belongs within the three constructs of law necessarily depends on where moral law is derived from.

Arthur Allen Leff, a professor of law at Yale, put it best in writing about this tension of *finding* versus *creating* moral laws:

"I want to believe—and so do you—in a complete, transcendent, and immanent set of propositions about right and wrong, *findable* rules that authoritatively and unambiguously direct us how to live righteously. ... [M]uch that is written about law today is understandable only in the context of this tension between the ideas of found law and made law[.]"[44]

The location where we concede or defend moral law to be within the whole of the law construct itself is critically important. If we understand moral law to be resigned to the realm of man-made law, we have conceded our ability to argue for objective truth without even realizing we have already lost the debate.

This concept of moral law being entirely subjective and fluid is incredibly dangerous because the logical end of an argument asserting that morals are confined to the philosophical and statutory constructs means that morals are therefore human constructs, human imposed, and humans have the right or even ability to negotiate them. We become the highest authority on morality and can change or apply morals at our sole discretion.

Under this view, morals would have no rigid, unchangeable absolutes or mandatory application. Morals could not be found or discovered as already existing, but would be relegated to being merely *agreed upon*.

The problem of where morality in law is derived from and the idea of legislating morality is particularly evident when we understand the assumptions that the two primary conflicting arguments are based in: Divine Law or the Social Contract Theory.

Divine Law

Divine Law, commonly referred to as Natural Law, is the principle that scientific *and* moral law is fixed, ordained by God, and "discoverable" by man. The terminology of "Divine Law" rather than "Natural Law" is preferred because the latter infers that the fixed, rigid principles of law only include the scientific construct and empirical laws of nature.

Moral law, as an absolute and objective law, could easily be excluded within this definition, according to secular theory. The term "Divine Law," on the other hand, specifically recognizes universal moral authority of an Author, Originator, and Creator of the law and therefore encompasses both recognized discoverable areas of law: science and morality.

Important to a proper understanding of the term "Divine Law" is distinguishing it from a theocracy or the principle of government that priests or church officials run the civil government in the name of God (or a god). As we will discuss further, the state as a government is distinct from the church—these are two separate spheres of government with distinct roles and jurisdiction. However, this does *not* imply a complete separation of church and state or adverse interests, as the courts and secular humanists have consistently tried to push.

As we will see when we analyze the text of the Founding Documents and other contemporary sources as "legislative history," the proper design of government is for the civil government and the church to be distinct but overlapping spheres and all under Divine Law, which includes moral law. We might analogize this principle to how the federal government is different in jurisdiction, but overlaps with and also works in harmony with the states (when functioning properly). So should the civil government and the church government function distinctly and in harmony together.

C.S. Lewis wrote,

> "Now this Law or Rule about Right and Wrong used to be called the Law of Nature. Nowadays, when we talk of the 'laws of nature' we usually mean things

like gravitation, or heredity, or the laws of chemistry. But when older thinkers called the Law of Right and Wrong 'the Law of Nature,' they really meant the Law of Human Nature. The idea was that, just as all bodies are governed by the law of gravitation, and organisms by biological laws, so the creature called man also had his law—with this great difference, that a body could not choose whether it obeyed the law of gravitation or not, but a man could choose to either obey the Law of Human Nature or to disobey it."[45]

Divine Law expressly states, "In the beginning, God[.]"[46] *Everything*, at its origin and inception, begins with God, including the law as a whole and the three constructs.

Divine Law presumes rational, objective limits and the legislative bodies of social government have no power to influence, redirect, redefine, ignore, or legislate against rigid laws of science and morality. God gives authority and enforcement to the law, and has firstly ordained all rigid, discoverable law, and secondly has given *limited* power to the three spheres of government (which He also ordained) to wisely legislate the law that is fluid and made *in accordance* with discoverable scientific and moral law.

These *three* spheres of God-ordained government are the social government, the church government, which we have already identified, and also the family government.

Consistent with Divine Law and God as the ultimate source of legitimate authority, the Apostle Paul discusses the legitimate role of civil government authority, established by God, in Romans 13:

"Let everyone be subject to the governing authorities, for there is no authority except that which God has established. The authorities that exist have been established by God. Consequently, whoever rebels

against the authority is rebelling against what God has
instituted, and those who do so will bring judgment
on themselves. For rulers hold no terror for those who
do right, but for those who do wrong. Do you want
to be free from fear of the one in authority? Then do
what is right and you will be commended. For the
one in authority is God's servant for your good. But
if you do wrong, be afraid, for rulers do not bear the
sword for no reason. They are God's servants, agents
of wrath to bring punishment on the wrongdoer.
Therefore, it is necessary to submit to the authorities,
not only because of possible punishment but also as a
matter of conscience. ...[F]or the authorities are God's
servants, who give their full time to governing."[47]

So then, these three spheres each have a different scope of limited,
Divine Law-derived authority and jurisdiction, and they occasionally
overlap and intersect with each other. A diagram of this idea looks
like this:

Fig. 3

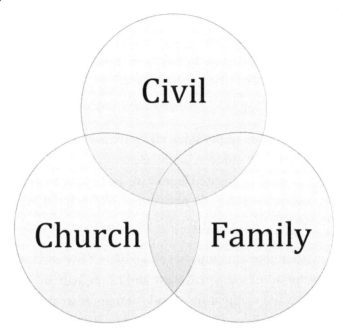

Three Spheres Diagram within Divine Law

Philosopher Alvin Plantinga examined the relationship between man and our ability to "discover" law:

> "God created both us and our world in such a way as there is a certain fit or match between the world and our cognitive faculties. The medieval had a phrase for it: *adequatio intellectus ad rem* (the adequation of the intellect to reality). The basic idea, here, is simply that there is a match between our cognitive or intellectual faculties and reality, thought of as including whatever exists, a match ***that enables us to know something***, indeed a great deal about the world—and also about ourselves and God himself" (emphasis added).[48]

This is *discoverable* law. Importantly, discoverable law's objective existence is not dependent on man's actual ability to know or discover it. We see through history and science that universal laws existed prior to man's actual discovery or knowledge of their existence. The world was round even when man believed it was flat, and subatomic particles existed before man's discovery they existed in 1897. "Discoverable" law then means law that is derived from something universal outside of man or his government.

Divine Law therefore supersedes all human-run government and man himself, and the three spheres of government, including civil law, must exercise their limited legislative and enforcement authority only to the extent that they do not contradict the fixed, unchanging laws, even within their overlap with each other.

Divine Law therefore encompasses all legislated law and is the source of authority for all of man-made law and necessarily includes moral law as objective and originating outside of man. If we understand that moral laws are equally as discoverable and unchangeable as scientific principles in that humans have zero authority to enforce statutorily constructed laws that are inconsistent with moral absolutes, the concept and terminology of Divine Law makes much more sense.

As professor and apologist William Lane Craig surmised, "If God exists, then objective right and wrong exist. God's own holy and perfectly good nature provides the absolute standard against which all actions and decisions are measured. His commands flow necessarily from His own moral nature and constitute for us our moral duties."[49]

Divine Law's authority and origins are derived from God Himself. The universe therefore has objective meaning and discoverable moral law. Society has value, and civil, church, and family government have limited powers that are derived from God's universal Divine Law.

Professor Richard Taylor writes in *Ethics, Faith, and Reason*, "The idea of moral…obligation is clear enough, provided reference to some lawmaker higher than those of the state is understood. In other words, our moral obligations…can be understood as those imposed by God.

This does give a clear sense to the claim that our moral obligations are more binding upon us than our political obligations[.]"[50]

Divine Law then provides the origin and basis for the law as a whole, and each of the three constructs of law, in the Divine Lawgiver. All legitimate authority must therefore be derived from God and no legitimate authority exists outside of God.

Social Contract Theory

In contrast, the Social Contract Theory is the idea that the law is fluid, ordained and authorized by man, and can be changed at whim by man. Moral and social laws have no inherent limits, but only that which the legislature sets, and collective society provides the authority and enforcement to the law. Majority and force of government therefore trumps, and any philosophical or statutory construct of law may be changed merely by the agreement and prevailing wind of the majority.

This theory posits there is no greater moral authority by which the laws of society must be conformed to on principle, but rather we tolerate some legislated morality simply for the protection of the society itself and its individual members. Law therefore functions as a crude cost/benefit relationship and society has no greater principled function than the benefits of membership.

Jean-Jacques Rousseau, in his work *The Social Contract*, argues, "man is born free" and that the only legitimate form of political government is the collective society where all members agree to the terms of the "social contract" and the end-goal is self-preservation of the individual. He defined the human individual as the state of man preexisting any social connections or relationships—a completely autonomous, disconnected, self-governing individual.[51]

Because mankind naturally does come to interact with each other, the only reason we need a government of any kind outside ourselves is to constrain these interpersonal relationships toward ultimate self-preservation. Rousseau did not acknowledge a legal construct outside man's original self that he was subordinate to, outside his own free will to assent to the "contract" of the state.

Pearcey further describes the utilitarian view of this form of state government and the major presupposition underpinning this contract—that social relationships do not contain any inherent moral value, but only value perceived and given by each individual subjectively.

> "In [Rousseau's] state of nature, human beings are autonomous selves, with no ties to others except those they choose for themselves. Virtually by definition, then, any relationships not a product of choice are oppressive—such as the biological bonds of family, the moral bonds of marriage, the spiritual bonds of the church, or the genetic bonds of clan and race. [...] The only social bond where individuals retain their pristine autonomy is the contract—because there the parties are free to choose for themselves how they wish to define the terms and the extent of their agreement. The terms are not preset by God, church, community, or moral tradition but are strictly voluntary. That's why Rousseau, Hobbes, and Locke all called for a state based on a "social contract." In it, all social ties would be dissolved and then reconstituted as contracts, based on choice. This was always presented in terms of liberating the individual from the oppression of convention, tradition, class, and the dead hand of the past."[52]

Interestingly, Rousseau goes on to argue that once this social contract is established, the grouping of the parties to the contract can be collectively termed the "Sovereign" and that single entity (sovereign) begins to act like an individual person. While each particular party to the contract has ideas of what is in his or her own best interests, this "Sovereign" acts on behalf of the general will and consensus of what is good for the whole of its members.

Majority rule becomes law and the force of the Sovereign trumps any individual party's will or interest—so each individual is no longer necessarily choosing by his own will. Rousseau's dictum is that the individual must be "forced to be free." In other words, the government Sovereign always claims to be acting within the individual's best and truest interests. Because there is no greater legal construct outside the Sovereign's own interpretation and construction of what it believes to be the best interests of the whole, we can understand how the Social Contract Theory begins to deteriorate quickly from a society driven by "the will and consent of the individual members" to a totalitarian regime of the Sovereign's rule.

Rousseau concedes that the Sovereign has legitimate authority only over matters that are of "public concern," but because the Sovereign's authority in this domain is absolute, we can see that an overreaching Sovereign can quickly and easily construe almost any matter as falling within the scope of "public concern." Without definite limits, such as the U.S. Constitution imposed on the government, "public concern" becomes a fluid term, subject to the whim of the acting Sovereign.

Totalitarian government swiftly is in place, overriding the "free man."

Rousseau even recommends the death penalty for parties to the social contract who are in perceived breach. This social contract state begins to have many philosophical similarities to the Capitol that acts as Sovereign in *The Hunger Games*—demanding total allegiance to the "benevolent" Sovereign and threat and force of death is effectuated for anyone speaking or acting against the presumed "best interests" acts and demands of the Capitol as Sovereign.[53]

The scientific construct is then the only force of law outside man's own autonomy, existing in the realm of the empirical world in which man finds himself. The scientific construct necessarily confines man against his will and supposedly inherent and absolute "freedom" that Rousseau describes. Social relationships and any other "constraint" on man that is outside his own autonomy must be assented to and is not discoverable under his theory, and Rousseau includes moral law within a socially defined construct, as he believes moral law is not necessary to a completely autonomous man.[54]

This social theory tree, of which one huge branch is the Social Contract Theory, has its roots in the greater scope of secular humanism as its substantive worldview.

Philosopher Jean-Paul Sartre in his *Essays in Existentialism* postulated that, "Man is nothing else but what he makes of himself. Such is the first principle of existentialism," and he also asserted that, "Life has no meaning a priori [reasoning or knowledge that is derived from rational and theoretical deduction rather than from observation or experience]… It is up to you to give it a meaning, and value is nothing but the meaning that you choose."[55]

The Social Contract Theory suggests exactly that—society has no inherent value or moral principles except that which is given to it by man's choice and mutual assent in this crude cost/benefit social relationship.

Professor and Veritas Forum speaker Dr. Mary Poplin summarized the central ideology of secular humanism: "The defining tenet of secular humanism is the belief that human reason is sufficiently reliable and just to guide the course of our lives—individually and collectively—without any consideration of divine authority[.] Secular humanists are optimistic about our abilities as a human community to come to consensus on civil and moral norms."[56]

Divine Law vs. Social Contract Theory

We see then that both Divine Law and the Social Contract Theory acknowledge that there *is* objective, discoverable natural law—at least in terms of the empirical world in which man finds himself. The main distinctions between these two theories of authority are where morality falls within the constructs of law and the origins of scientific law and moral law—a universal objective divine authority or man's subjective social agreement?

So then, defining "Natural Law" as only containing the scientific construct and leaving mankind free to negotiate his own social contractual value is not inconsistent with the Social Contract Theory. Most secular humanists would still agree that we obviously are not free to legislate against an empirical scientific law, regardless of how we feel about that or whether we "believe in" or even know about scientific principles. Congress may declare that gravity no longer exists, but we would laugh at the absurdity of such a declaration.

Simply by virtue of our existence in the universe, we realize that the limitations of our social government are necessarily dependent on our authority to enforce our statutorily constructed laws. We must extend this same reasoning into *all* law's authority, begin with the law outside man's ability to negotiate or devise—this discoverable law—and logically deduct civil government's legitimate authority from this initial premise.

As Poplin further explains, "The reason the scientific method is so reliable and productive is that we live in a law-governed universe rather than one that operates on random or changing laws. In addition, our minds, being made in the image of God, are specially fit to study and understand the world."[57]

Because of this a priori assumption, based on a clear logical deduction from discoverable law and that there is a Divine Lawgiver, the Social Contract Theory *is* wholly inconsistent with Divine Law. We are *not* free to legislate and enforce inconsistently with discoverable moral laws any more than we are free to disobey scientific laws or suffer the immediate cause and effect consequences if we try, which also happens to be a scientific law in and of itself.

Arthur Allen Leff reasoned, "*We* are not doing the defining [of moral law]. Our relationship to God's moral order is the triangle's relationship to the order of Euclidean plane geometry, not the mathematician's. We are intrinsically morally defined, constituted as beings whose adultery is wrong, bad, unlawful. Thus, committing adultery in such a system is 'naturally' bad only because the system is supernaturally constituted."[58] And discoverable!

Consider then the completely opposite conclusions about law (its origins, rationale, authority, enforcement, and interpretation) at which we arrive, depending on whether we base our understanding of law in either Divine Law or the Social Contract Theory rooted in secular humanism:

Fig. 4

	DIVINE LAW	SOCIAL CONTRACT THEORY
ORIGIN	God	Man
RATIONALE	Fixed, objective, discoverable	Fluid, subjective, made
AUTHORITY	God's sovereignty	Man's agreement
ENFORCEMENT	Moral Law God's supremacy	Statutory law Sovereign's power of force
INTERPRETATION	Unchangeable: Consistent with fixed law (scientific and moral)	Changeable: Dependent on whim of social majority/ Sovereign

Divine Law vs. Social Contract Theory Chart

Importantly, there are two relevant questions when understanding the legal basis of authority in Divine Law versus the Social Contract Theory.

First, is the Social Contract Theory *ever* a legitimate source of authority? Craig succinctly answers this complex question borrowing from the logical conclusions of the philosophy of Sartre and of Camus, who argued that if a Divine Lawgiver does not exist, then all of life, including man himself, is absurd:

> "The absurdity of life without God may not prove that God exists, but it does show that the question of God's existence is the most important question a person can ask. No one who truly grasps the implications of atheism [including secular humanism, the premise of the Social Contract Theory] can say "Whatever!" about whether there is a God. Now when I use the word *God* in this context, I mean an all-powerful, perfectly good Creator of the world who offers us eternal life. If such a God does not exist, then life is absurd. That is to say, life has no ultimate meaning, value, or purpose. These three notions— meaning, value, and purpose—though closely related are distinct. *Meaning* has to do with significance, why something matters. *Value* has to do with good and evil, right and wrong. *Purpose* has to do with a goal, a reason for something. My claim is that if there is no God [and therefore no Divine Law], then meaning, value, and purpose are ultimately human illusions. ... This point is worth underscoring, since it's so frequently misunderstood."[59]

Craig's argument is true for the meaning, value, and purpose of law. Without an eternal, objective Divine Lawgiver, man is left to debate the absurdity of the very concept of civil government and the law itself.

Why shouldn't the individual man, as Rousseau contemplated, revert back to his natural state and rebel against the very idea or contractual relationship of a totalitarian government where he finds himself no longer a consenting individual, but under the regime of a substituted Sovereign?

If civil government's majority force as the answer to man's inevitable social relationships is the sole basis for law, this is not actually a *legitimate* source of authority. We see examples of government force that we know instinctively and from a moral basis were not legitimate powers. The most obvious example is Hitler and the Nazi regime. Though Hitler had the weight of force and the German government authority behind him for his actions, no one would argue credibly that this was legitimate because the German government, by force and social contract, all agreed it was legitimate.

Further, legitimacy as a concept would be self-defeating because there is no fixed objective standard by which all law must conform. No law would be inherently more legitimate than another. All law would be debatable, and man's natural state of complete autonomy would necessitate that there is no objective, fixed right or wrong, but only a myriad of differing opinions and wills of each man.

The concept of authority also becomes meaningless and is replaced with power of force from the majority as Sovereign. Because its highest source of authority is derived from man's whim and majority, the Social Contract Theory cannot ever be a legitimate source of authority.

This concept of legitimacy in law as a whole only makes sense if also understood through the lens of Divine Law. Legitimacy is lawfulness and inherent authority by virtue of being authorized or in accordance with truth. Expressed another way, the law is only legitimate if it conforms to a valid, rightful, and appropriate authority. For example, we have socially constructed laws that forbid vigilante justice—the idea that individual members of society may seek retribution or restitution outside the procedural justice system.

The rationale behind this law is that any actions outside the justice system are illegitimate and an invalid appropriation of authority. For this reason, American statutes also criminalize impersonation of a police officer. An individual member of society must be duly authorized to enforce social law. Any other attempt at enforcement lacks authority.

The very concept of the social construct of law presupposes that there is legitimate authority and illegitimate authority. However, if the highest source of authority is man and his government, then any law becomes debatable and we are back to lacking any rational basis for arguing *any* source of legitimate authority or, for example, that Hitler's government was objectively illegitimate authority. Hitler had the force of majority, so that made his government legal under a Social Contract Theory end rationale.

The Social Contract Theory cannot logically provide a rational basis for *any* legitimate authority.

More specifically relevant to the question of Constitutional interpretation is the second question: Upon which source of authority is the U.S. Constitution founded? We actually do not even have to resolve the first question if we know definitively the source of authority for the U.S. Constitution is Divine Law. (If the source were the Social Contract Theory, then the first question would be necessary and would precede debates about moral law and its place in government legislative action.)

However, because Divine Law necessarily excludes the Social Contract Theory, if we can show that American government derives its authority from a Divine Law basis, then the Supreme Court and the Judiciary or any other branch of American government is not free to make or interpret law within the statutory construct that is not in accordance with Divine Law.

That law necessarily would be *illegitimate.*

In this same way, any statutory construct of law must be confined to the extent of its legitimate authority, which necessarily includes moral law when we are within the framework of Divine Law as authority. Going back to the hypothetical of Congress outlawing the law of gravity, we can now see the parallel absurdity of legislating against the unchangeable, discoverable laws of morality.

The only difference is one of empirical observation and Divine Law's enforcement. For His own sovereign reasons, God allowed physical laws to be discoverable and immediately enforced (cause and effect), whereas moral laws are discoverable but enforced at God's timing, discretion, and ultimate providence.

This most important point, however, cannot be ignored: just because we do not empirically observe the enforcement mechanism of moral laws empirically as with scientific laws *does not* mean that moral laws are any less discoverable, constant, unchanging, and outside man's authority to manipulate or negotiate.

There is a cause and effect to moral law, even if we do not readily and empirically observe the effect after the breach of a moral law.

Finally, legitimacy also comprises two important legal concepts: *lawfulness* and *legality*. Lawful means to be in accordance with morality and science (discoverable law). Legal means to be in accordance with civil government (made law). These two terms are fundamentally different in that what is or is not lawful is unchanging, whereas what is or is not legal may change. Morality and science inherently contain aspects of lawfulness and unlawfulness that are unchanging, immutable, and eternal.

We see now that legitimacy is vitally important in law within the philosophical construct (logic and values of law), the statutory construct (man–made law), and what we have now come to realize as both the scientific *and* moral construct (discoverable law). Without legitimacy in these areas, the law itself would cease to have any meaning, value, or significance.

Important to our topic of U.S. Constitutional law and interpreting the Founding Documents, we now understand what "the law" is and its authority and legitimacy from the perspective of a lawyer (and therefore from the perspective of the Founders), and hence we can begin to unpack the text of the legal documents themselves and determine the legitimate authority to which the Founders directly appealed in penning the Founding Documents and in setting up a new government for our nation.

Secular humanist theorists will argue that the U.S. Constitution is merely a social contract—having no basis in any law or authority outside of the "consent of the governed," a phrase they argue shows that the Founders appealed to the authority of the people (mankind itself) for the authority and legitimacy of the law.

The logical conclusion of this foundation is that *even if* the Founders' original intent and a fixed, objective meaning implies only one interpretation of the U.S. Constitution, it ultimately is immaterial because the government as Sovereign is free to act in the best interests of the people as a whole and free to liberally construe and amend the U.S. Constitution whenever and however it sees fit. We also see now why arguments for a moral basis to the U.S. Constitution cannot survive solely appealing to the faith of the Founding Fathers.

Even appealing to the U.S. Constitution then becomes a token reference and without any actual authority. And is this not exactly what we are seeing today with decisions like *Obergefell* and even in the past few decades with *Roe v. Wade*?[60]

The secular humanist position says the nine Supreme Court justices currently comprising the American Sovereign are the highest source of judicial review and are free to rule according to the majority whim of the current culture, amend and alter the U.S. Constitution as they see fit, and recreate it at will because it is merely a contract having no greater authority or legitimacy.

We will see, however, that the text of the Founding Documents themselves clearly and textually shows that the Founder lawyers appealed directly to Divine Law as the sole legal basis for American government's authority and legitimacy, and this legal basis necessitates and requires a moral, objective Constitutional interpretation.

CHAPTER 4

THE FOUNDING DOCUMENTS: A PURPOSEFUL HIERARCHY

"The general principles on which the fathers achieved independence were the general principles of Christianity. I will avow that I then believed, and now believe, that those general principles of Christianity are as eternal and immutable as the existence and attributes of God."[61]

- John Adams

As author and professor William Lane Craig wrote, "An event without a context is inherently ambiguous."[62]

This is especially true for a major historical event, such as the ratification of the U.S. Constitution. Considered in total isolation and without understanding the plain meaning of legal terms of art, we might read the text as confusingly as we might read chapter 17 of a novel. We would be proceeding without the proper context of the setting, character development, and events that are important to the story.

For legal documents, we need to understand not only the text of the document itself, but also the *context*. Even deriving the plain meaning and considering *only* the text of a legal document is still done in context. We still have the threshold presumptions of context—that the interpretation is taking place within American courts and under American laws and American laws' understood meaning and in American English. The context provides the backdrop and necessary presuppositions to a correct interpretation of a document.

The legal term of art for these presuppositions is "basic assumptions."

Consider the differences in the basic assumptions of a contract that has been entered into by parties in China during the Ming Dynasty in the 1400s versus a contract formed in the United States in the 2000s. It is immediately apparent the basic assumptions will be inherently different for the Chinese Contract than for the American Contract, because the context of these documents and the applicable law is very different. Therefore the meaning will also be inherently predicated on the basic assumptions of legal terms commonly understood to those parties and lawyers.

So, we must consider not only the basic assumptions for the U.S. Constitution, but consider the whole context during which this legal document was formed. This includes an understanding of the foundation of the U.S. Constitution and its interrelationship with the Declaration of Independence.

The two most important legal documents in American history produced the legal effect of separating from English government, establishing a new political sovereignty (independence) and new government system, and setting forth the rules, regulations, and supreme law of that new governmental system. These two documents are the Declaration of Independence and the U.S. Constitution of the United States of America. They have often been collectively called "The Charters of Freedom."

One other important set of documents is the Federalist Papers, which comprise a significant legislative history and rationale for the new nation and the U.S. Constitution, but do not have any legal effect or actual binding authority.

To illustrate the legal effect of these documents and their relationship to each other, consider the following pyramid of the Founding Documents as a hierarchy:

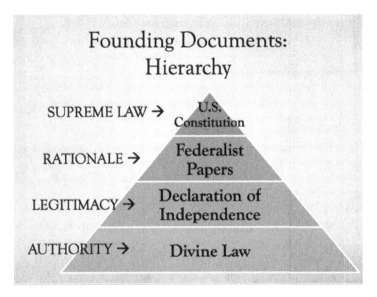

Founding Documents: Hierarchy

This hierarchy is vitally important to understand the relationship of the Founding Documents to each other and how they are necessarily structured within a legal and worldview framework.

Without Divine Law as the cornerstone and providing the foundational level of authority, the Declaration of Independence would not have legitimacy in announcing the new political sovereignty of the United States. The U.S. Constitution as Supreme Law is built upon the legitimate authority of Divine Law and the Declaration of Independence, and without understanding that key concept, context, and this hierarchical relationship, we cannot properly understand the rationale of the U.S. Constitution, establishing new form of government in conformance to its legitimate authority, nor can we properly understand how to interpret and apply the U.S. Constitution today.

The chief problem in Constitutional interpretation and jurisprudential concerns we have seen in recent American history is two-fold:

First, we have allowed the secular narrative to erode our Divine Law authority without addressing the *foundational* misconception of this narrative and without understanding the Founding Documents as a hierarchy. Second, when we as Christians argue for objective morality, we generally enter the debate at the top of the pyramid (at best) or address each moral or statutory legal issue head-on (worse) or have allowed the secular agenda to redefine the entire context of the U.S. Constitution and replace the true legitimate authority with a Social Contract Theory (at worst).

When we argue for a morally based U.S. Constitution, if there is no mutually understood rational basis and foundation for this appeal, secular theorists are dismissive, saying that this effort is merely an attempt to advance a certain religion and they cite to "separation of church and state" and the First Amendment. Even more shockingly, most evangelical Christians *agree* with them.

We must understand and articulate the legitimate basis of our appeal to Divine Law as the only correct foundation for Constitutional interpretation.

Nancy Pearcey summed up the faith-based misconception perfectly when she wrote:

> "Instead of offering a distinctly biblical perspective on the current political culture, many evangelicals virtually equated spiritual liberty with political liberty. ... In other words, the American Revolution was only a halfway measure: We've thrown off political tyranny, now we must throw off ecclesiastical

tyranny. [Quoting Baptist minister and political writer Elias Smith] 'Venture to be as independent in things of religion, as those which respect the government in which you live.'" ... What was emerging in the populist branch of evangelicalism was a new individualistic, even atomistic, view of the church. ... The church was no longer an organic community into which one was received, and certainly not a spiritual authority to which one submitted. Rather, it was a collection of equal, autonomous individuals coming together by choice. ...[T]hat last sentence should set off loud bells in your mind: Populist evangelicals were sounding the same note as the early social contract theorists— Hobbs, Locke, and Rousseau—who regarded social structures as the creation of sheer choice, formed by the consent of autonomous individuals living in a 'state of nature.' After the revolution, social contract theory gained enormous plausibility among Americans, because it seemed to describe what they were actually experiencing. Even Christians echoed similar themes in their views of church."[63]

The secular narrative shrewdly cuts off the U.S. Constitution from its source of authority and its historical context and then reinterprets its concepts to support their humanistic conclusions.

Christians blindly follow these amoral ideas without realizing what is actually happening, believing we are *better off* with a so-called "separation of church and state" that is actually rooted in secular humanism and nowhere in the Constitutional hierarchy or in the Divine Law interaction of spheres of government.

We have no idea what this concept really means, where it comes from, or what its practical effect has been, until it is too late and we have profoundly lost significant moral ground on life, liberty, religious freedom, marriage, and culture.

First, we must understand the real debate and how to articulate it to a culture that has lost all moral grounding and the standard of Divine Law. Our Founding Documents and all of our legitimate, unalienable rights are grounded in and can only be derived from the unique, Judeo-Christian concept of man's inherent dignity as a human being made in the image of God, endowed with reason, rationality, free will, common sense, an eternal soul, and the capacity to discover.

Second, we have not properly educated our culture and ourselves on the true historical context and legal implications of the Founding Documents and how to engage the debate on the foundational level. In any kind of debate setting, whoever defines the terms usually wins. If we allow the secular narrative to continue to creatively redefine "life" and "liberty" and "equality" and reconstruct the Constitutional foundations as being rooted in the Social Contract Theory, we have already lost the debate before we have said a word.

How many of us have engaged a secular humanist that has been dismissive of our appeal to morality because they "don't believe in God" and therefore invalidate our argument for a moral U.S. Constitution on that basis?

We *must* educate ourselves in the true source of legitimate authority and the meaning of these Founding Documents and be prepared to start at the foundation of the hierarchy rather than be distracted by the top-level outcome of the secular humanist worldview on social issues. We must not let the secular narrative define the terms of the debate and shut out a theistic worldview and Divine Law on subjective beliefs. This is objective truth.

As we will see when delving into the text of the Declaration of Independence itself, and then up the pyramid through the Federalist

Papers and finally into the U.S. Constitution, the Founders derived the legitimacy of the Declaration of Independence upon the foundational authority of Divine Law—not the Social Contract Theory. These legal documents only make sense and are properly understood in context when we begin with the foundation of Divine Law and its authority.

Remember, Divine Law presumes that law is fixed, ordained by God, and "discovered" by man, presumes that law has rational, objective limits that humans are bound by, and Divine Law specifically recognizes the moral and legal authority of an Author and Originator of the Divine Lawgiver.

Now that we have discussed Divine Law and understand the inherent and significant differences between Divine Law and the Social Contract Theory, we will understand the basic principles of Constitutional interpretation and how to correctly understand the meaning of a document.

Then, we will examine the text of the Declaration of Independence itself and ascend the pyramid to see that the Founders as lawyers appealed directly to the authority of Divine Law to legitimize the Declaration of Independence's legal effect and set the stage for ratifying the U.S. Constitution as our form of government.

CHAPTER 5

UNDERSTANDING ORIGINALISM: PRINCIPLES TO CORRECT TEXTUAL INTERPRETATION

"I consider the foundation of the Constitution as laid on this ground: That 'all powers not delegated to the United States, by the Constitution, nor prohibited by it to the States, are reserved to the States or to the people.' To take a single step beyond the boundaries thus specially drawn around the powers of Congress, is to take possession of a boundless field of power, no longer susceptible of any definition."[64]

- Thomas Jefferson

Before we study exactly how the Supreme Court has reinvented and redefined the U.S. Constitution to advance its progressive secular humanist agenda, we first must understand the correct and legitimate way to interpret not only the U.S. Constitution, but also any text. There are uniform principles for reading any text and understanding its true meaning from the perspective of original intent, rather than perceiving any fluid or subjective meaning.

While certainly the U.S. Constitution is an important and significant document, the point in this chapter is that the U.S. Constitution is not a *unique* document in the sense that it has special rules of interpretation unlike any other ordinary legal document.

The Founders, as lawyers, wrote the U.S Constitution as supreme law of the land, exactly like many other nations have drafted and ratified national constitutions throughout the course of human history. The U.S. Constitution is unique in its structure of government and its recognition and assent to Divine Law as its legitimate basis of authority, but it is not different whatsoever as a *written document* than any other constitution.

Similarly, this book is unique from any others published because of what it contains, but it is exactly the same in its identity as a written *book*. The reader opens this book to understand the ideas conveyed herein by the author—not to presume what the author might be saying, or attempt to confer a "fluid" meaning. When discussing this book or any other book in a group setting, debate centers around agreement or disagreement with the ideas set forth in the book—not what each reader has independently decided the book is saying.

Meaning is vitally important to communication. Language, both spoken and written words, is the key weapon in our communication arsenal. Without objective meaning imputed to a given word and series of words, why bother to read at all?

Misunderstanding or miscommunication occurs when the speaker has a different understanding of imputed meaning than the listener. Fine-tuning language and the speaker choosing words that he or she knows the listener will understand provides clear communication.

Part of a lawyer's training is to learn the specific meaning imputed to the legal terms of art, and employ these legal terms in the precise manner that another lawyer will read or hear and understand the intent of the author. Similarly, the Founder lawyers had the background and training on precise legal terminology and terms of art so that they were capable of employing these legal terms in a constitution so precisely that every lawyer thereafter could read and understand their exact intent.

The U.S. Constitution is in plain English, but is also written containing legal terms of art. Any lawyer educated in the meaning attributed to these terms will readily understand the plain meaning of the U.S. Constitution. Yet America at large has been sold on this idea that the U.S. Constitution is such a unique document that legal scholars cannot know for certain the plain meaning and therefore application of the plain meaning is virtually impossible, and must be left to the superior judgment of the Supreme Court.

This is absurd. We need legislators, judges, and especially Supreme Court members who will not usurp their authority and recognize that the plain text of the U.S. Constitution is the supreme law of the land, not a majority's subjective interpretation.

So how does a lawyer read the U.S. Constitution? Beyond understanding the concrete, determinable meaning of the legal terms of art, the doctrine of Originalism provides several keys for correct interpretation of *any* written text, including the U.S. Constitution.

Importantly, each of these principles must be taken *together* in order to arrive at correct meaning. Often, one principle is taken without the others and an incorrect interpretation is arrived at on partial truth. These principles work together to provide an accurate understanding of textual meaning.

Principle 1: Authorial Meaning

Any written text has an author—the person (or persons) who wrote it. An author chooses particular words and phrases to communicate a specific meaning to the reader. Similarly to a conversation where the speaker chooses his or her words in order to convey a thought to the listener, an author does the exact same thing through written communication.

The first key to understanding the meaning of a text is to realize that the author establishes meaning. Not the reader. A reader may ultimately disagree with the author, have a different opinion or viewpoint, but the reader is not free to substitute his or her *own* meaning into the text.

The most common form of miscommunication happens between two people (the author and the reader; the speaker and the listener) when the reader/listener misunderstands or incorrectly perceives the intent of the author.

This happens all the time between husband and wife or parent and child. How many times have you heard a loved one's words and interpreted them in a way that later that loved one said, "No, that's not what I meant!"

Meaning is inherently vested with the originator or author of the text.

It's worthy to note here that occasionally the author's intent is for the reader to substitute his or her own meaning into the text. But importantly, this subjective meaning is specifically conveyed to the reader prior to reading the text—and such meaning is still the *author's* choice and intent. The presumption of communication is that meaning remains with the author.

The Founders, as lawyers, chose specific words and phrases to convey a very specific meaning to ratify their agreement as to the powers delegated to federal government, and so specifically that later generations and anyone else not actually physically present the Constitutional Convention would understand the plain meaning. The meaning is vested in the intent of the Founders—not the readers 225 years later.

If meaning is not originating from the author of the text and is assigned to the reader without the author's consent, then meaning itself becomes totally meaningless.

Consider how ridiculous communication would become if you could not say anything to your loved one without giving them the power to interpret it however they want, regardless of what you meant through your choice of words.

If your loved one can choose to interpret the words "I love you" as "I hate you," what is the point of actually saying anything? Words would cease to mean anything and there would be no such thing as communication. Communication inherently requires understanding of the author's intended meaning by the reader.

Meaning *must* logically remain the sole province of the author. For Constitutional interpretation, the threshold principle is that the Founders themselves are the originators of the meaning of the U.S. Constitution. Their original meaning trumps any perception or interpretation of the reader.

Principle 2: Exclusive Original Meaning

For any text to have any genuine meaning, it by necessity must have one original meaning. If the text could have multiple meanings, then actual communication is entirely lost.

This original meaning therefore logically excludes any *other* meanings.

Meaning not only is vested exclusively with the author, but also is exclusive in singularity—it is not relative, dependent on the reader. Original intent does not change with the identity of the reader. Authorial intent does not change for a reader who says, "Well that's not what I think it means" or "This interpretation doesn't mean anything to me."

Meaning is exclusive and vested with the author, regardless of whether the reader comprehends the intended meaning. Intended meaning as a factual assertion is not negated in any way by the failure of the reader to accurately interpret or understand.

Now certainly a speaker can convey specific words to one specific listener knowing that the listener will understand a special meaning. However, there is still only *one* original authorial intent. In this same way, the Founders authored a document that contained specialized terms of art that had very specific legal meaning to other lawyers. This does not negate the fact that there is still one original, exclusive meaning.

Principle 3: Objective, Concrete and Binding Meaning

This concept is often referred to by legal scholars as the "plain meaning" of the text. Unless otherwise defined as a specific, not readily inferred meaning, the words mean what they appear to mean to a reasonable person.

If an author states, "I am an American," the plain meaning is that the author is a citizen of the United States of America.

Often, readers try to infer or ascribe a symbolic meaning to the text and read into it something that goes far beyond the text and that the author did not intend in that specific text. Christians often see this misunderstanding of meaning exemplified in the ways biblical text is often interpreted. We go beyond the objective, concrete and plain meaning of biblical text and instead assign a symbolic or super-spiritual meaning.

In our example, a reader who attempts to ascribe symbolic meaning to the author's statement, "I am an American," may assert that this means the author is conveying a sense of pride in country and standing firm on the ideals of liberty and the melting pot of diversity! This symbolic meaning will not only quickly go far beyond the original intent of the author, but will also have no clear stopping point for what meaning is excluded. Almost anything can be "read into" the text when interpreted symbolically. This becomes incredibly dangerous for meaning.

In the same way, the Supreme Court has taken various words and phrases from the text of the U.S. Constitution and ascribed a symbolic meaning to squeeze out of the text the legal outcome they want.

This is a terrible way to interpret any text. If we begin with the conclusion and look for the words that can somehow fit our pre-designated and desired interpretation, we aren't actually reading the text for meaning; we are trying to fit the text into our own meaning through symbolism.

As one legal author wrote,

> "Originalism is championed for a number of fundamental reasons. First, it comports with the nature of a constitution, which binds and limits any one generation from ruling according to the passion of the times. The Framers of the Constitution of 1787 knew what they were about, forming a frame of government for "ourselves and our Posterity." They did not understand "We the people" to be merely an assemblage of individuals at any one point in time but a "people" as an association, indeed a number of overlapping associations, over the course of many generations, including our own. In the end, the Constitution of 1787 is as much a constitution for us as it was for the Founding generation."[65]

The U.S. Constitution has a plain, *binding* meaning. The reader is not free to assign words and phrases or any open-ended symbolic meaning to fit his or her own purposes. This is inconsistent with the rational, logical purpose of meaning.

Principle 4: Contextual Meaning

Words are not said in a vacuum. Communication always has context: identity of the author, time and place of communicating, and other factors that bear upon context.

Context is "the circumstances that form the setting for an event, statement, or idea, and in terms of which it can be fully understood and assessed."[66]

To fully understand and assess the author's intended meaning, context is critical. We saw the example in Chapter 4 of how the context changes the basic assumptions of a contract, depending on the context where the contract was written. As we discussed, it is immediately apparent the basic assumptions will be inherently different for the Chinese Contract than for the American Contract, because the context of these documents and the applicable law is very different. Therefore, the meaning will also inherently be predicated on the context.

Consider the phrase, "Bring that over here!" Out of context, we have no idea what this means. We might think we know a part of the meaning—the author is likely communicating to the intended listener to bring whatever "that" is to the author. But without context, we simply can't know the full meaning. Now, consider if we knew the context to be a classroom, and a student had just exclaimed, "Teacher, I found a pencil on the ground!" With this additional contextual information, we now immediately know exactly what the original statement, "Bring that over here!" means.

Context is important on both micro and macro levels. On the micro level, context is important to understand the word within the sentence, the sentence within the paragraph, the paragraph within the chapter, and the chapter within the whole document. A single phrase or sentence taken out of the whole can be misconstrued or misunderstood as meaning something entirely different than the author intended.

Context on the macro level is identifying the scope and purpose of the document. It is necessary to understand the whole document within the time it was written, authorship identity, purpose for the document, relation to other contemporaneous writings (such as a number in a series or placement in a hierarchy), etc.

All of these contextual clues provide more data points to navigate the text and pinpoint the precise meaning.

Principle 5: Meaning through Consideration of the Whole

This principle establishes that we must take the meaning of the *whole document*, rather than attempt to derive meaning from select words and phrases out of context.

Doing so is referred to as "proof-texting," which is the concept of building meaning around one phrase or word. Many judicial opinions take a passage of law or Constitutional text out of context to make a point that goes well beyond the actual meaning of that passage. We see this in many biblical verse references as well—the person reciting the passage is seeking for the listener to take *only* the plain meaning of the words recited, without regard to what came before or after in the passage.

To truly understand the author's original intended meaning, we have to take the entirety of the document(s) as a whole. Again, similarly to biblical text, we cannot understand the true meaning of biblical doctrine if we simply take out one phrase of any book of the Bible and build a doctrine around that verse. Unfortunately, we see that happening often in churches, and this is an incorrect way to read the text of Scripture as much as it is an incorrect way to read the text of the U.S. Constitution.

Meaning must be considered within the context of the whole document. One of the most stark examples of this is in the modern era is when the Supreme Court took the phrase "separation of church and state" entirely out of context and built an entire doctrine around that phrase.

Not only does that phrase not actually appear anywhere within the text of the U.S. Constitution, but it is also taken out of context from the whole letter from Thomas Jefferson to the Danbury Church. Yet the current secular mantra has taught this doctrine as originating from the U.S. Constitution itself.

When we begin reviewing other Supreme Court decisions and "doctrines" that are supposedly legitimate interpretations of the U.S. Constitution, keep in mind this principle of proof-texting and how the Supreme Court has taken tiny phrases out of the U.S. Constitution or other texts and substituted its desired meaning for the *actual* meaning, when the Founding Documents are taken as a whole.

So then, taking the five principles together, we have to give deference to the original, exclusive, authorial meaning—even if we disagree with the author's meaning. We must give deference to the original meaning even if we wish it were something different. We can legitimately debate the merit of an author's idea or statement, but we cannot ascribe a different meaning to the idea than the one the author intended.

The Founders knew this to be true in the context of legal documents. For example, two parties litigating a contract dispute must give deference to the plain meaning of a written contract, even if one party wishes that the provision that essentially says that they owe the other party monetary damages actually said something else. The reason the legal system relies on the validity of contracts to form agreements is because there is objective meaning—both parties have adequate assurances that there is concrete, known meaning to their agreement and can rely on a future court also understanding that meaning.

If the U.S. Constitution didn't actually *mean* anything concrete and determinable, then what is the point of having a supreme law of the land? If we can't know for sure what the text means, or it changes depending on the "time and place in society," then we do not actually have a supreme law of the land, but rather a "king" figure in the Supreme Court that is above the law and can say and do anything it wants for any reason it wants.

This is exactly why the U.S. Constitution is so important as a written document and an Originalist meaning is absolutely critical.

When we allow the U.S. Constitution to be a "fluid" document, we are replacing all of these rational principles with the whim of a majority's interpretation that is above the plain meaning. American government specifically established government to be under the written U.S. Constitution as a fixed, rational, meaningful document.

What is amazing about the inconsistency of liberal legal scholars is that their argument asserts the U.S. Constitution is somehow the only legal document that is so "fluid," yet those same legal scholars (many of whom are judges) would never accept "fluidity" as a defense for contract interpretation or even other legislative interpretation. No lawyer comes into a contract dispute and argues that the plain terms of a contract are "fluid."

We cannot accept fluidity as a defense for incorrect and fantastical Constitutional interpretation either.

As we delve into the text of the Founding Documents, keep in mind these five principles, their interrelationship to each other, and consider the meaning of the text in light of these principles.

CHAPTER 6

THE DECLARATION OF INDEPENDENCE

"In the chain of human events, the birthday of the nation is indissolubly linked with the birthday of the Savior. The Declaration of Independence laid the cornerstone of human government upon the first precepts of Christianity."[67]

- John Quincy Adams

The Declaration of Independence is the legal document that effectively created the independent political sovereignty of the United States' colonies. The Declaration of Independence was not simply a public relations statement, a personal letter from the Founders to the King of England, or any other type of written document that did not inherently mandate a legal effect.

The Declaration of Independence, like a legal document in today's courts, had a practical significant legal effect, and in order to accomplish this mandate, it systematically drew from Divine Law authority to state a legal cause of action (list of grievances against the English government for ceasing to function in the legitimate role of government), legal justification for separation, and its intrinsic legitimacy (independence and sovereignty).

The Declaration of Independence has been aptly nicknamed the "Great American Complaint," and other similar variations, because its legal effect was to render a lawful and legal Complaint (another legal term of art) against England's government, and thus justify a new nation's sovereignty and reconstituting a legitimate form of government.

The contents of the Declaration of Independence are shown by listing the colonial grievances against King George III and England and by asserting certain Divine Law rights—natural, moral, and legal rights—including the unalienable rights bestowed by Divine Law, the people's right to reform government when the current government ceases its legitimate role, separation from the current government, and independent sovereignty.

This "Great Complaint" begins by drawing its authority from a law even greater than the supreme law and ruler of England—Divine Law's fixed, unchanging, discoverable law.

The text of the Declaration of Independence begins,

> *"When in the Course of human events, it becomes necessary for one people to dissolve the political bands which have connected them with another, and to assume among the powers of the earth, the separate and equal station to **which the Laws of Nature and of Nature's God entitle them**, a decent respect to the opinions of mankind requires that they should declare the causes that impel them to separation.*
>
> ***We hold these truths to be self-evident**, that all men are created equal, that **they are endowed by their Creator with certain unalienable Rights**, that among these are Life, Liberty, and the pursuit of Happiness—That to secure these rights, Governments are instituted among Men, deriving their just powers from consent of the governed. That whenever any Form of Government becomes destructive of*

these ends, it is the Right of the People to alter or to abolish it, and to institute new Government, laying its foundation on such principles and organizing its powers in such form, as to them shall seem most likely to effect their Safety and Happiness" (emphasis added).[68]

The Declaration of Independence goes on to submit the list of grievances against England, its government, and its ruler, pointing out the inconsistences of the government with the people's unalienable rights, and then concludes with this appeal to Divine Law's authority:

*"We, therefore, the Representatives of the united States of America, in General Congress, Assembled, **appealing to the Supreme Judge of the world** for the rectitude of our intentions, do, in the Name, and by Authority of the good People of these Colonies, solemnly publish and declare, That these United Colonies are, and of Right ought to be Free and Independent States. [...] **And for the support of this Declaration, with a firm reliance on the protection of divine Providence**, we mutually pledge to each other our Lives, our Fortunes, and our sacred Honor"* (emphasis added).[69]

We can see clearly that Divine law is the authority and legal basis for American sovereignty and everything that came after. Thus, the Founders began building the pyramid hierarchy with the foundation of Divine Law as the authority, and the Declaration of Independence enumerated the legitimacy for American sovereignty. See again the hierarchy:

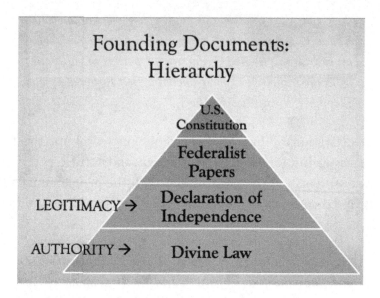

Founding Documents: Hierarchy (Authority, Legitimacy)

Some historians and lawyers argue that the Declaration of Independence has no legal effect and should be considered merely an historical document because the United States was not yet formed, and because the Continental Congress did not speak on behalf of the States within the Union.

However, this is a flimsy and transparent attempt to disconnect the U.S. Constitution from its legal basis and its legitimate authority for existing as the supreme law of the land.

Although the ratification of this Complaint was through a consensus of the Continental Congress on behalf of the Colonies, the Colonies were the represented parties within the Complaint or "Declaration" and *had already* formed themselves into a union of states, thus becoming the "United States of America" and later establishing the supreme law of the land (the U.S. Constitution). The identified parties are "the thirteen united States of America" and "these United Colonies," and the conclusion shows that the signatories are the legal representatives of these united states.

The logical progression of the new American sovereignty was first to declare a legal separation from England's government, and *then* to form a new government and supreme law of the land, **under** the authority that first gave the legally justifiable basis for separation. The states had already formed a new union, and without the Declaration of Independence, the U.S. Constitution would have had no legal authority over the states or as a substitution for English law.

The historians who seek to relegate the Declaration of Independence to a mere historical document without any legal authority do so out of a fallacious attempt to cut off the legal effect and the appeal to divine authority that is plainly evident in the text of the Declaration of Independence.

One university historian said,

> "Just as each age re-writes history according to its own values and beliefs, so men and women interpret words like those of the American Declaration of Independence in a way which reflects their own ideas and aspirations. It's important to remember that our views today are as limited and specific to our time and society as Jefferson's were to his. … The job of the historian is not to judge Jefferson, but to understand why he penned the Declaration of Independence in the way he did."[70]

It's an accurate insight that we must view the Declaration of Independence in historical context, but the Declaration of Independence was not Jefferson's philosophical rant. We are not studying the text of the Declaration of Independence as a mere intellectual curiosity or solely for historical knowledge that has no bearing on America today. There was a specific legal purpose and legal effect for each of the Founding Documents. This is the "why." Similarly, the U.S. Constitution was not created in a vacuum, nor was the Continental Congress a "task force" agent of England to draft and design a new government on behalf of England (thus deriving legitimate authority from England's government).

We have to understand the Founding Documents in their historical context and also their legal context. If the U.S. Constitution is built upon the foundation of the Declaration of Independence, which it absolutely was, then the secular interpretation of an amoral U.S. Constitution also absolutely fails.

The U.S. Constitution only has its legitimate authority as Supreme Law *because of* the Declaration of Independence. The Declaration of Independence only had its legitimacy because of the authority of Divine Law. Cutting off the U.S. Constitution from its roots also cuts off its legitimate authority and leaves bare the U.S. Constitution to stand on its own and leaves the text open to reconstruction from a Social Contract Theory perspective.

Secularists have tried first to sever the U.S. Constitution from its roots, and then systematically and continuously to attempt to reinterpret the U.S. Constitution as a "fluid" document, stripping it of any actual, meaningful supremacy and catering to the whim of the current majority (through the rule of nine justices), diametrically opposed to the written, legally plain original intent of the lawyers that comprised our Founding Fathers.

Consider how different the pyramid and Founding Documents hierarchy becomes when the U.S. Constitution stands on its own as a social contract, separated from the Declaration of Independence (which is relegated to a mere "historical document" and not even present in the structure of civil government), and thereby the Social Contract Theory is unable to provide any legitimate authority for a new sovereignty and new government.

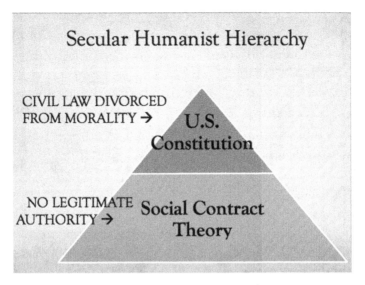

Secular Humanist Hierarchy

Let's look more closely at the text of the Declaration of Independence and what each term of art means from these lawyers, and why the Founders' legal basis was firmly rooted in Divine Law as the United States' authority, not the Social Contract Theory.

The first sentence of the Declaration of Independence says,

> *"When in the Course of human events, it becomes necessary for one people to dissolve the political bands which have connected them with another, and to assume among the powers of the earth, the separate and equal station to* **which the Laws of Nature and of Nature's God entitle them,** *a decent respect to the opinions of mankind requires that they should declare the causes that impel them to separation"* (emphasis added).[71]

What is this saying in legal terms? The five lawyers we have previously identified as comprising the Declaration Committee (Jefferson, Adams, Franklin, Sherman, and Livingston) knew that in order for the Declaration of Independence to have any legal authority to go *against* England's then-current authority, it must appeal to a **higher** legal authority. Otherwise, a rebellion and separation from English governmental authority would not be justified or legitimate.

These lawyers knew that all governments are under the authority of Divine Law and that it is God, not any man-made government, who gives fundamental rights to mankind. A government only has the powers and authority that Divine Law gives it.

This is one of the major premises of the Magna Carta—the idea that the king was *under* the law; he was not the supreme law itself. It is the same idea for any king or government head, even if such government is a representative or democratic government—all government is under the supreme law of the land, and that law is under Divine Law which is fixed and unchanging.

Thus, acting as the legal power of attorney and representatives of the people of the unified states, the Founder lawyers began their legal complaint and declaration with citing the legal authority. They said, in legal terms, that when a government is so significantly in breach of its legitimate authority **given to the government** by God through Divine Law, the people of the states are actually equal in the eyes of God as those in power in the government (kings, parliaments, etc.) and have the divinely bestowed Right to separate. The "Laws of Nature and of Nature's God" *entitle* them to separate.

This was a legitimate revolution, as the Founder lawyers appealed to the authority of God Himself and of Divine Law. The legal legitimacy of the Declaration of Independence's separation and establishment of a new sovereignty was premised squarely and solely in Divine Law.

Apart from the discoverable, fixed, unchanging laws of God, the Declaration of Independence had no inherent authority. History is full of rebellions and revolutions, many of which were not legitimate or justified and depended entirely on whether the legal basis to which the revolution appealed was authoritative and legitimate—*not* whether the collective judgment of subsequent history confirmed or denied its legitimacy through popularity or majority (which are simple pseudonyms for a social contract theory basis), or even whether or not the revolution itself was ultimately successful.

Divine Law is the only legal authority that is legitimate for the American Revolution and reestablishment of a new government. If, as Rousseau surmised, the Sovereign entity that all individual parties have consented to govern is necessarily acting in the best interests of the whole, the patriots of the Revolution would not have been ethically free under a Social Contract Theory to disregard the will of the then–sovereign (English rule) for their own individual ideas and self–interest.

After asserting the legal authority by which the Declaration of Independence is legitimate, the Founder lawyers of the Declaration of Independence then continue to incorporate and appeal to Divine Law principles and its legitimate rationale:

> "***We hold these truths to be self-evident***, *that all men are created equal, that* ***they are endowed by their Creator with certain unalienable Rights***, *that among these are Life, Liberty, and the pursuit of Happiness—That to secure these rights, Governments are instituted among Men, deriving their just powers from consent of the governed. That whenever any Form of Government becomes destructive of these ends, it is the Right of the People to alter or to abolish it, and to institute new Government, laying its foundation on such principles and organizing its powers in such form, as to them shall seem most likely to effect their Safety and Happiness*" (emphasis added).[72]

What are the lawyers saying here? Driving these principles from Divine Law's discoverable laws, the Founders understood that there are "truths" that are "self-evident" or *findable*.

Notice that their appeal is not to a new social contract. The Founders did not say, "We hold our own truths to be man-made and self-ratified through the contractual power of the states' free will, having no other higher authority to which we appeal." They did not say, "We hold our own power of contract equal to England, and we are free to separate from that contract and enter into our own by our own authority."

The lawyers representing the United States at its very conception specifically stated their appeal to discoverable, unchanging, self-evident laws that are endowed not by a social contract government, but endowed by the **Creator**, and because of Him the authority for the Declaration of Independence is found within certain unalienable Rights.

How amazing of our founding lawyers both to recognize this and to put it in writing so that we can *know* they recognized Divine Law as our nation's authority!

Note the absolute legal terms: "truths," "self-evident," "endowed by their Creator," "certain," "unalienable," "Rights." The Declaration of Independence is *not* an historical document without legal authority, nor is it a new social contract between the states. The Declaration of Independence is a legal complaint, citing the highest authority of Divine Law, and a fixed, moral authority. The Founders, as lawyers, set forth in plain legal terms their basis for authority, in specific legal language that is plainly understood by other lawyers.

The Declaration of Independence then goes on to describe the purpose and legitimate form of government as a sphere within and *under* Divine Law's authority.

> *"That to secure these rights, Governments are instituted among Men, deriving their just powers from consent of the governed."*[73]

In other words, the sole legitimate purpose of government is to secure for individuals under Divine Law's authority the unalienable rights bestowed upon mankind through the discoverable laws of nature— including morality. Governments derive their legitimate power not from a social contract or from a government's own forcible power, but from consent of the people who already possess these rights.

In the same way, an individual patient, who already has power over his or her own medical decisions, may consent to give that medical power of decision-making to a doctor or group of doctors that the patient believes will act in his or her best interests to secure the patient's life, but may revoke that power if the medical professional ceases acting in the patient's best interest or securing the patient's physical health and life. Government acts as a representative of people *solely* to secure the unalienable rights that Divine Law has already given each person.

Government therefore is powerless to abridge these rights, and is not in any sense the provider of these rights. Government is merely the safeguard of the people's unalienable rights. Unalienable, as a legal term, means "unable to be taken away or given away by the possessor."[74] The Founders expressly recognized that the only legitimate role of government was to secure Divine Law principles for the people.

So then, the Declaration of Independence continues,

> *"That whenever any Form of Government becomes destructive of these ends, it is the Right of the People to alter or to abolish it, and to institute new Government, laying its foundation on such principles and organizing its powers in such form, as to them shall seem most likely to effect their Safety and Happiness*[.]"[75]

The Founder lawyers then go on to demonstrate exactly how King George III and the English government had indeed become destructive of "these ends"—the only legitimate purpose of government. They list nearly thirty grievances against the English government that had not been rectified and brought back into conformance with Divine Law.

Appealing again to the unalienable rights and Divine Law principles, the Founders state that it is an inherent, God-given *right* of the people to alter or abolish government, and institute a new form of government in order to return that government to conformance with Divine Law.

We now see how the Founders ensured that England, as their government predecessor, and the future established government of the United States, including our contemporary government officials (elected and appointed), knew from their legal appeal that their authority and legitimacy for the Declaration of Independence and separation from England's government was rooted squarely in Divine Law.

After listing the substance of their complaints and grievances of behalf of the people in the States, the Founders then concluded with a reassertion of their direct appeal to Divine Law's authority:

> "*We, therefore, the Representatives of the united States of America, in General Congress, Assembled,* **appealing to the Supreme Judge of the world** *for the* **rectitude** *of our intentions, do, in the Name, and by Authority of the good People of these Colonies, solemnly publish and declare, That these United Colonies are, and of Right ought to be Free and Independent States. [...]* **And for the support of this Declaration, with a firm reliance on the protection of divine Providence,** *we mutually pledge to each other our Lives, our Fortunes, and our sacred Honor*" (emphasis added).[76]

These lawyers could not have made their authority more clear—they appealed exclusively and unambiguously to "the Supreme Judge of the world" for the *rectitude* of their intentions within this legal document. "Rectitude" means "morally correct behavior" or "righteousness."[77]

As Samuel Adams, signatory of the Declaration of Independence and ratifier of the U.S. Constitution, reasoned during his tenure as Governor of Massachusetts,

> "I conceive we cannot better express ourselves than by humbly supplicating the Supreme Ruler of the world...that the confusions that are and have been among the nations may be overruled by the promoting and speedily bringing in the holy and happy period when kingdoms of our Lord and Savior Jesus Christ may be everywhere established, and the people willingly bow to the scepter of Him who is the Prince of Peace."[78]

The Founders specifically incorporated morality within Divine Law and understood that moral law was findable, discoverable, and fixed within "the Laws of Nature and of Nature's God." **Everything** outflowing from the Declaration of Independence that concerns the newly established government of the United States in any way is logically and legally subject to this declaration of Divine Law authority.

As James Madison wrote,

> "We the Subscribers say, that the General Assembly of this Commonwealth have no such authority [against Divine Law]: And that no effort may be omitted on our part against so dangerous an usurpation, we oppose to it, this remonstrance; earnestly praying, as we are in duty bound, that the Supreme Lawgiver of the Universe, by illuminating those to whom

it is addressed, my on the one hand, turn their Councils from every act which would affront his holy prerogative, or violate the trust committed to them: and on the other, guide them into every measure which may be worthy of his blessing, may redound to their own praise, and may establish more firmly the liberties, the prosperity and the happiness of the Commonwealth."[79]

This is the sole legitimate role of government.

"Let every soul be subject to the governing authorities. For there is no authority except from God, and the authorities that exist are appointed by God."[80]

Having appealed to the unalienable rights and the Divine Law principles and authority in the text of the Declaration of Independence, the Founders stated that it is an irreversible, unalterable, immutable, God-given right of the people to alter or abolish government and institute a new form of government in order to return that government to conformance with Divine Law—the sole legitimate role of government.

Importantly, the Founders specifically recognized that abolishing or revolting against established government for any *other* reason apart from exercising the Divine Law rights and returning government to its original scope and specific purpose would be illegitimate revolution.

Government does have legitimate civil authority over individual citizens and acting in civil disobedience against the government (the philosophical idea that) must be carefully exercised, and generally only as a last remedial option, once all other forms of respectfully petitioning the government to return to conformance with its legitimate authority under Divine Law have been fully exhausted.

Notably, the Declaration of Independence also elucidates the Founders' understanding of this very principle. Immediately after declaring the sole legitimate purpose of the government and the unalienable right of the people to alter or abolish it, the Declaration of Independence provides the balance of civil government authority to this right of the people and justifies why the colonies believed that separation and abolishing their government was the only and last option.

> *"Prudence, indeed, will dictate that Governments long established should not be changed for light and transient causes; and accordingly all experience hath shewn, that mankind are more disposed to suffer, while evils are sufferable, than to right themselves by abolishing the forms to which they are accustomed."*[81]

The Founders here were acknowledging that the most extreme act of civil disobedience—abolishing government—was not to be done lightly and for "light and transient causes." They recognized that there are many instances where the people may disagree with government or even feel abused by government, but while these "evils" (as they term government abuse) are sufferable, generally the people should defer to governmental authority, petition the government, and seek to change the government from within.

This is consistent with Paul's discussion of the legitimate role of civil government's authority in Romans 13. It is not until we have exhausted all options *and* the abuses are so evil that Divine Law necessitates that the people exercise their legitimate authority of civil disobedience and abolish the government in order to institute a new government consistent with Divine Law.

The "evils" that the Founders put forth to not only justify their decision but also compelled them as a *duty* to separate from England were, they argued, "design[ed] to reduce them under absolute

Despotism," they had long suffered and had petitioned British government and the King without any remedy from the government for their grievances.

> *"But when a long train of abuses and usurpations, pursuing invariably the same object evinces a design to reduce them under absolute Despotism, it is their right, it is their duty, to throw off such Government, and to provide new Guards for their future security. Such has been the patient sufferance of these Colonies; and such is now the necessity which constrains them to alter their former Systems of Government. The history of the present King of Great Britain is a history of repeated injuries and usurpations, all having in direct object the establishment of an absolute Tyranny over these States. To prove this, let Facts be submitted to a candid world."*[82]

The Declaration of Independence then goes on to list the Facts and allegations—approximately 30 of them. Then it continues:

> *"In every stage of these Oppressions We have Petitioned for Redress in the most humble terms: Our repeated Petitions have been answered only by repeated injury. A Prince whose character is thus marked by every act which may define a Tyrant, is unfit to be the ruler of a free people."*[83]

Then is described the appeal to the British legislature for justice, which,

> *"They too have been deaf to the voice of justice and consanguinity."*[84]

The Founders rested the final judgment of the justification of their exercise of right to separation in the hands of the "Supreme Judge of the world," a direct appeal to God and Divine Law for their moral and civil authority for civil disobedience—the legal effect of the Declaration of Independence. This was not an action taken for disagreement with government that might be characterized as "light and transient" causes of action.

> "...with a firm reliance on the protection of Divine Providence, we mutually pledge to each other our Lives, our Fortunes, and our sacred Honor."[85]

CHAPTER 7

THE FEDERALIST PAPERS

"And on that grace, a sinner has the highest encouragement to repose his confidence, because it is tendered to him upon the surest foundation: the Scripture, testifying that we have redemption through the blood of Jesus, the forgiveness of sins, according to the richness of His grace. I have a tender reliance on the mercy of the Almighty, through the merits of the Lord Jesus Christ."[86]

- Alexander Hamilton

Having exercised justified civil disobedience as a duty in the context of the circumstances they confronted, the Founders were now left to shape a new form of government. We see through the text of the Declaration of Independence itself that they recognized civil government might take on different and equally legitimate *forms*, so long as the legitimate *effect* of the government (securing the people's Divine Law rights) was actually ensued.

The Founders recognized that Divine Law inherently requires that a legitimate form of government protect, preserve, and secure the unalienable rights of the people; however, Divine Law does not inherently require one specific form of government in order to accomplish that security.

We see many different forms of legitimate and illegitimate governments throughout history, just as we see many different examples of legitimate and illegitimate revolutions and rebellions. The Founders agreed and assented through the Declaration of Independence what Divine Law has defined—what the purpose of legitimate government is and is not. The Founders demonstrated why the then–current English government was not fulfilling that purpose, effectively and illegitimately stripping the States of their unalienable rights, in a manner entirely inconsistent with Divine Law principles.

The Founders therefore, under a common goal of creating a legitimate form of government that best accomplished securing of rights to the people, passionately debated what structure of government should be established for the United States. These debates and the rationale for each Founder's thoughts and perspectives are largely preserved in the Federalist Papers, the Anti–Federalist Papers, personal letters from the Founders, the Annals of Congress, and the records kept of the Constitutional Convention, among other contemporaneous documents.

Importantly, the Founders were not convening under the banner of a Social Contract Theory (convening for the purpose of assenting to a common government contract founded in secular, illegitimate authority), but rather previously published the Declaration of Independence, which appealed to Divine Law as the legitimate authoritative legal basis.

Some legal scholars assert that because the Articles of Confederation were already ratified prior to the Constitutional Convention, the delegates to the convention were acting outside the scope of their authority as delegates.[87] However, this theory has little merit because the Articles of Confederation were never intended as anything except a temporary measure.

The Constitutional Convention and all of the rationale and debates about the various "nuts and bolts" and design of the government were from varying viewpoints on how to best *implement* the only legitimate form of government—securing these unalienable rights, endowed by the Creator through the Laws of Nature and of Nature's God.

As James Madison wrote in the Federalist Papers,

> "'[T]he equal right of every citizen to the free exercise of his religion according to the dictates of conscience" is held by the same tenure with all his other rights. *If we recur to its origin, it is equally the gift of nature*; if we weigh its importance, it cannot be less dear to us; if we consider the "*Declaration of those rights which pertain to the good people of Virginia, as the basis and foundation of government*," it is enumerated with equal solemnity, or rather studied emphasis" (emphasis added).[88]

Madison, the lawyer, was asserting that the very basis, foundation, and legitimacy of government is to declare the equal rights of the individual citizen with origins in nature or Divine—*precisely* what the Declaration of Independence accomplished.

Yet a common misinterpretation of the phrase "consent of the governed" (from the Declaration of Independence's preamble) and of the nature of the Constitutional Convention itself is the belief that the Founders were discussing the U.S. Constitution as a contract between the States and that the signing of the U.S. Constitution as Supreme Law meant both ratification on the Founders' own authority and the individual states consenting to a new social contract.

Secularists who seek to cut off the U.S. Constitution from its actual authority and dissociate the Declaration of Independence from its legal effect on America's origins largely drive this misconception by the rewriting of American history through their own humanist narrative.

The term of art "consent of the governed," is in context describing the legitimate role of government. As the Founders indicated in the Declaration of Independence when using that term, whenever any form of government becomes destructive of the *discoverable*, Divine Law given unalienable rights rather than merely being the mechanism of securing those rights, the one of those very rights is the right of the people (those governed) to alter government or abolish the current form and establish a new government to which they consent will fulfill its legitimate role.

The Founders understood and actually documented in the written text of the Declaration of Independence that the people themselves are the greatest and most significant check on the legitimacy of any form of government, with the standard of Divine Law authority. When the people rightly and provably believe that the government is no longer securing their rights or acting according to legitimate authority, the people have the absolute and inalienable right to cease their consent, through altering or recreating their government.

This delicate balance between government as an ***authority over*** the people and the people as the ***consenting constituency*** of the government is exactly what the Founders debated, and what we saw that Paul was referencing in Romans 13.

Obviously, the government would have no actual authority if it were so easily altered or abolished based on the whim of the people without proof. But the government would also have too much illegitimate authority if it could not be altered at all and the people could not revoke their consent. Though on face it does not seem intuitive, in reality the idea of actual consent of the people is wholly inconsistent with the logical conclusions of the Social Contract Theory.

As we discussed in Chapter 3, any social contract that is not bound by any other outside and higher legal construct ultimately ends in a totalitarian form of government and the people are left helplessly subject to the Sovereign. Certainly the Founders were clear that the unalienable rights to individuals were bestowed by a higher law than merely an agreement by all parties that they want such rights.

The Founders had an entirely different premise than the Social Contract Theory for the existence of government—that there is preexisting, findable, discoverable law in "the Law of Nature" and that government is established *subordinate* to those unalienable rights and exists solely to protect those higher, God-given rights for each individual within its governmental scope.

Thus, we see the rationale for the amazing dichotomy the Founders understood between the people's rights and authority and the government's legitimate authority in preserving those rights that eventually became the ratified text of the U.S. Constitution as Supreme Law governance of the United States.

The only logical conclusion for the Founder's own premises of the individual and government from the text of the Declaration of Independence is completely different and antithetical to Rousseau, Locke, and Hobbes' premises and is *necessarily* derived from the Divine Law theory.

James Madison, a Founder lawyer, wrote,

> "We hold it for a fundamental and undeniable truth, 'that Religion or the duty which we owe to our Creator and the Manner of discharging it, can be directed only by reason and conviction, not by force or violence.' The Religion then of every man must be left to the conviction and conscience of every man; and it is the right of every man to exercise it as these may dictate. ***This right is in its nature an unalienable***

right. It is unalienable; because the opinions of men, depending only on the evidence contemplated by their own minds, cannot follow the dictates of other men: It is unalienable also; because what is here a right towards men, is a duty towards the Creator. It is the duty of every man to render to the Creator such homage, and such only, as he believes to be acceptable to him. This duty is precedent both in order of time and degree of obligation, to the claims of Civil Society. ***Before any man can be considered as a member of Civil Society, he must be considered as a subject of the Governor of the Universe***: And if a member of Civil Society, who enters into any subordinate Association, must always do it with a reservation of his duty to the general authority; much more must every man who becomes a member of any particular Civil Society, do it with a saving of his allegiance to the **Universal Sovereign**. We maintain therefore that in matters of Religion, ***no man's right is abridged by the institution of Civil Society***, and that Religion is wholly exempt from its cognizance. True it is, that no other rule exists, by which any question which may divide a Society, can be ultimately determined, but the will of the majority; but it is also true, that the majority may trespass on the rights of the minority" (emphasis added).[89]

This dichotomy can be summarized into the basic logical premises that we see the Founders knew and textually expressed through the Declaration of Independence that are necessary for a legitimate form of government:

1. Government must secure the unalienable rights endowed by our Creator.
2. Government must not abridge these unalienable rights.

3. Government must exercise legitimate authority in securing and not abridging these rights, subject to "the laws of nature and of nature's God."

These three premises, taken *together*, are what the Founders asserted through the Declaration of Independence. Each is necessarily as important as the other to create the proper balance of the legitimate role of government. We can see through the logical conclusions of these premises that they are not inconsistent with each other or incoherent separately. They provide the most basic assertion of what our government must look like.

Logically then, the Founders wanted the form of government that would provide the optimal outcome, consistent with the principles of the proper role of government. Government is necessary to secure rights. But because it is also true that there will never be a perfect government, there will be some level of government failure either to secure unalienable rights or to abridge them.

The Founders acknowledged this: if men were perfect, no government would be necessary to secure unalienable rights. But because government is necessary to govern imperfect men, government run by imperfect men will therefore also be imperfect.

James Madison pondered this, writing in Federalist No. 51:

> "It may be a reflection on human nature, that such devices should be necessary to control the abuses of government. … If men were angels, no government would be necessary. If angels were to govern men, neither external nor internal controls on government would be necessary. In framing a government which is to be administered by men over men, the great difficulty lies in this: you must first enable the government to control the governed; and in the next place oblige it to control itself."[90]

The principle of optimal outcome states that there is one available alternative (among all available alternatives) that will lead to a better outcome than the remaining alternatives. This is a principle in decision theory, and an example of this is financial investment. Financial investment involves two competing principles: minimizing risk while maximizing gain. There cannot be gain without some risk, so the optimal outcome is to choose the alternative among all financial investment decisions that is the smallest risk for the biggest gain.

In government political theory, these are the three premises of government the Founders stated, and inserted into an optimal outcome equation, it would be expressed like this: The optimal civil government is the form of government that *maximizes* securing rights and *minimizes* abridging them, while operating within the scope of legitimate authority.

Again, we know that there is no perfect form of government that will secure rights 100 percent while abridging them 0 percent. So the optimal outcome is as close to 100 percent in securing while simultaneously as close to 0 percent abridging, *and* consistent with the third principle: still exercising legitimate authority. This is the balance of powers to limit government authority, and the balance between government authority and consent of the governed.

We can readily point to historical examples of how governments have not achieved this optimal outcome either by too much securing with too much abridging, not enough securing with too much abridging, etc., or utilizing methods of securing or abridging, or both, that constitute illegitimate authority (Hitler's government would be an example).

Thus, these forms of political governments (like England) that were shown to have stepped so far *outside* of the scope of legitimacy (not just being slightly off from optimal) then justified civil disobedience or revolution.

Remember the text of the Declaration of Independence:

> *"That whenever any Form of Government becomes destructive of these ends, it is the Right of the People to alter or to abolish it, and to institute a new Government, laying its foundation on such principles and organizing its powers in such form, as to them shall seem the most likely to effect their Safety and Happiness. Prudence, indeed, will dictate that Governments long established should not be changed for light and transient causes; and accordingly, all experience hath shewn, that mankind are more disposed to suffer, while evils are sufferable, than to right themselves by abolishing the forms to which they are accustomed."*[91]

Here, a very important point must be made: simply because the Founders disagreed on slight variations in this political equation and how best to achieve the optimal outcome, that does not mean that they disagreed on the legitimate role of government, its principles for optimal outcome, or its only source of legitimate authority.

In fact, we see in the Federalist Papers and other contemporaneous writings and of course in the Declaration of Independence itself, these three principles of government were *never controverted.*

The Federalist Papers lend keen insight into the Founders' rationale for a legitimate, optimal system of government and further evidences their direct appeal to the authority of Divine Law. Accordingly, we can properly place this series of contemporaneously written (and therefore preserved) debates on the Founding Documents hierarchy as founded in Divine Law's authority and the Declaration of Independence's legitimacy, providing the rationale and "legislative history" for the U.S. Constitution to be rooted in:

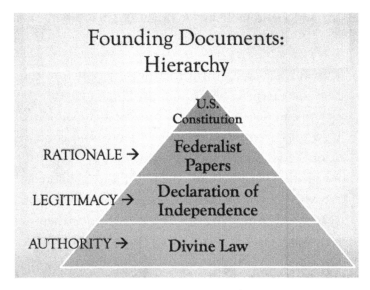

Founding Documents: Hierarchy (Authority,
Legitimacy, Rationale)

The Federalist Papers consist of 85 articles and essays authored by
Alexander Hamilton, James Madison, and John Jay (again, all lawyers).
These Papers promoted the ratification of the U.S. Constitution and
demonstrated the Founder lawyers' rationale for the text of the U.S.
Constitution—the Supreme Law of the land.

Remember, the Founders had already published and asserted their
Declaration of Independence of Independence and through that
legal document, transparently and overtly declared the foundational
authority for this new sovereign government in Divine Law. The
Federalist Papers were now discussing the best and most effective
way to accomplish their professed role of government—securing
the unalienable rights of the people, endowed by their Creator
(Divine Law).

In Federalist No. 84, Hamilton argues that it is unnecessary to add
the Bill of Rights to the U.S. Constitution, precisely because the
Founders agreed that these unalienable rights were endowed by

Divine Law and unalterable by any form of government. Hamilton argues,

> "I go further, and affirm that bills of rights, in the sense and extent in which they are contended for, are not only unnecessary in the proposed constitution, but would even be dangerous. They would contain various exceptions to powers which are not granted; and on this vary account, would afford a colorable pretext to claim more than were granted. For why declare that things shall not be done which there is no power to do? Why for instance, should it be said, that the liberty of the press shall not be restrained, when no power is given by which restrictions may be imposed? I will not contend that such a provision would confer regulating power; but it is evident that it would furnish, to men disposed to usurp, a plausible pretense for claiming that power."[92]

What is Hamilton discussing here? The Bill of Rights is the collective name for the first ten Amendments to the U.S. Constitution, written by James Madison and ultimately ratified by the signatories over Hamilton's concerns in Federalist No. 84. The Bill of Rights specifies textual prohibitions on the government.

Importantly, the Bill of Rights does not confer or grant benefits *from* the government *to* the people.

A common misperception of the Amendments is the theory that "I have a right to free speech because the First Amendment says I do." This assertion presupposes that the U.S. Constitution (i.e. the government) is the benefactor and giver of these rights, and therefore the inverse of this assertion would also have to be true—if the First Amendment did not say that I have the right to free speech or if the government did not give it, I would not have it.

This misperception was exactly what Hamilton wanted to avoid. He was concerned in Federalist No. 84 that a Bill of Rights was not only unnecessary, but would actually be dangerous, precisely because of this inverse assertion. If the U.S. Constitution/Bill of Rights were construed by future government leaders that it does not say that a person has free speech (or his example, freedom of press), then people would believe that they did not in fact have that right.

Curiously, this sounds exactly like our government today. This is the legal difference between a right being "textually granted" (given by the government through the U.S. Constitution) versus an unalienable right (given by our Creator through Divine Law).

Hamilton argued that because the Founders had *already* declared that certain rights are unalienable, according to Divine Law, it would be unnecessary to declare that again within the U.S. Constitution. He believed that it was dangerous because people could start looking to the U.S. Constitution's text and line-itemed rights as being rights simply because they are listed, rather than realizing that their rights are endowed by their Creator, regardless of their textual inclusion in the U.S. Constitution.

Hamilton foresaw the possible illegitimate government claim from "men disposed to usurp, a plausible pretense for claiming that power"—that if the *U.S. Constitution* was the basis for granting these rights to the people, the government-established interpreters of the U.S. Constitution could revoke, amend, or abolish these rights and, in Hamilton's own words, having a "plausible pretense" for claiming this illegitimate authority.

The Declaration of Independence had already stated, in accordance with Divine Law, that these unalienable rights of the individual people were above any governmental power to inhibit, and that the sole legitimate function of government is to secure those rights.

Hamilton forewarned, "They [bills of rights] would contain various exceptions to powers which are ***not granted***; and on this vary account, would afford a colorable pretext to claim more than were granted. For why declare that things shall not be done which there is no power to do?"[93] (emphasis added).

His primary concern was two-fold: that the people would begin to see their unalienable rights as *granted*—bestowed by the government, which therefore could rescind or constrain those rights—and that because of this misconception and line-iteming certain rights, the government would itself be able to misconstrue the text under a "colorable pretext" and claim more regulatory power over these rights than was granted.

Hamilton was arguing in legal terms, understood by his lawyer peers. "Colorable pretext" is another term of art. A "colorable" claim in law means a claim that is seemingly valid or having a genuine basis in law or fact—a plausible legal claim or claim that is strong enough to have a reasonable chance of being valid if the legal basis is generally correct or evidence proves it to be true. A "pretext" in law means a false purpose or motive alleged in order to hide the real purpose, motive, or reason for doing something.[94]

So Hamilton was arguing that the government would illegitimately assert a false purpose or motive as a pretext for a plausible reason to usurp its authority and claim more power than is actually granted by Divine Law.

How clearly he understood this warning!

This is *precisely* what our current government has systematically accomplished through the secular narrative of first eroding the foundation in Divine Law authority and replacing it with the Social Contract Theory. Once our power of government comes not from our Creator but from our own authority and the government is free to act as Sovereign in the "best interests" of the people without any moral restrictions, and morality has been relegated to a philosophical "idea," the men Hamilton described as "disposed to usurp" would then assert a plausible, colorable pretext to claim more authority than is actually granted.

James Madison expressed a similar concern in Federalist No. 51, commenting on the necessity for separation of powers and checks and balances on government, lest the rights of the people be usurped:

> "In order to lay a due foundation for that separate and distinct exercise of the different powers of government, which to a certain extent is admitted on all hands to be essential to the preservation of liberty... [t]he interest of the man must be connected with the constitutional rights of the [government agency]. It may be a reflection on human nature, that such devices should be necessary to control the abuses of government."[95]

Even the Founders like Madison, who argued in favor of a Bill of Rights, understood that the government must understand its inherent limitations, purpose, and scope so as not to usurp Divine Law authority. Madison understood that Divine Law did not allow the government to act as ultimate benevolent Sovereign on behalf of the general welfare and best interests of society as whole, subverting its own judgment for the consent of the governed, as in a Social Contract Theory design.

In a letter to James Robertson, Madison discussed the text of the U.S. Constitution, which he had at that point already advocated for and signed. He wrote on April 20, 1831, "With respect to the words 'general welfare,' I have always regarded them as qualified by the detail of powers connected with them. To take them in a literal and unlimited sense would be a metamorphosis of the U.S. Constitution into a character which there is a host of proofs was not contemplated by its creators."[96]

Madison also wrote the following in agreement with the Divine Law justification for the Declaration of Independence: "The free men of America did not wait till usurped power had strengthened itself by exercise, and entangled the question in precedents. They saw all the consequences in the principle, and they avoided the consequences by denying the principle. We revere this lesson too much soon to forget it."[97]

Madison, like Hamilton, understood that the powers of government were qualified, limited, and finite.

The words "general welfare" did not mean literally *anything* that the government as Sovereign decided on behalf of the people, like in a Social Contract Theory framework. Madison argued, as Hamilton did, that the U.S. Constitution was **under** the superior authority of Divine Law and for the U.S. Constitution to be a fluid, changing document based on promoting the "general welfare" in a Rousseau theory sense would be, in Madison's own words, "metamorphosis of the U.S. Constitution" which "was not contemplated by its creators."

The Founders, including Hamilton and Madison, agreed on the legitimate basis of Divine Law—the debate, in contrast, centered on the *form* of government that would best align with Divine Law principles. The Founders could not have been clearer about the role, scope, and subordinate legitimacy of government to Divine Law authority.

· CHAPTER 8 ·

THE UNITED STATES CONSTITUTION

*"The great, vital, and conservative element in our system
is the belief of our people in the pure doctrines and the
Divine Truths of the Gospel of Jesus Christ."*[98]

- Congress, 1854

Now we clearly see the legal basis and moral foundation of the U.S. Constitution as electing the particular form of government, ratified for the sole purpose of being consistent with Divine Law authority and unalienable rights given by the Creator and Supreme Judge of the Universe.

The U.S. Constitution was not created in a vacuum, as a mere contract instituted by the self-proclaimed power and will of the Founders as rebellious social contract theorists, and *must not* be understood or construed apart from its authority in Divine Law, legitimacy in the Declaration of Independence, and rationale evidenced within Divine Law, the Declaration of Independence, and the many contemporaneous documents that comprise the Federalist Papers and legislative history of the formation and framing of the U.S. Constitution.

Even though the U.S. Constitution is the supreme civil law of the United States, the text of the U.S. Constitution provides *only* the "nuts and bolts" of the form of government eventually agreed upon by the Founders to best secure Divine Law morals and rights. We see this in the Founding Documents Hierarchy:

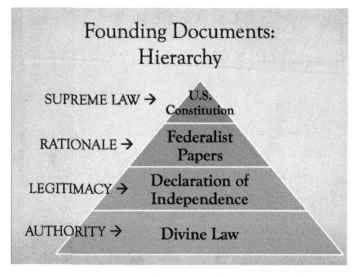

Founding Documents: Hierarchy (Authority, Legitimacy, Rationale, Supreme Law)

What is known as the Preamble to the U.S. Constitution begins,

> *"We the People of the United States, in Order to form a more perfect Union, establish Justice, insure domestic Tranquility, provide for the common defence, promote the general Welfare, and secure the Blessings of Liberty to ourselves and our Posterity, do ordain and establish this Constitution for the United States of America."*[99]

In context with what has already been stated through the Declaration of Independence, we understand these words in the light of Divine Law's authority and the Declaration of Independence itself. Since the role and legitimate purpose of government had already been declared, it was the *form* of government to which this Preamble speaks. It speaks not to a Social Contract Theory or contractual relationship between the states, but is a *continuation* of the rationale first affirmed in the Declaration of Independence, founded upon Divine Law.

Now the "People of the United States" (then having no government), stated through this Preamble that this is the form of legitimate government that has been determined to best effect the role and purpose of a legitimate government—a "more perfect Union."

The foundation of the U.S. Constitution cannot reasonably be divorced from its roots, nor can any legitimate interpretation of the U.S. Constitution be inconsistent with Divine Law, biblical morality, or abridge our unalienable, discoverable rights endowed by God.

Framed by 55 delegates to the Constitutional Convention, it is the final product of the legal basis, authority, legitimacy, and rationale for the new nation of the United States. 32 signers of the U.S. Constitution, an almost 60 percent majority of them, were lawyers. It is a legal document and its sole purpose is to preserve unalienable rights under the legitimacy of the Declaration of Independence and God's vested authority in civil government to structure and form itself in accordance with Divine Law.

Remember, the U.S. Constitution's only legitimacy and authority is founded in Divine Law—neither government itself, nor the government acting as Sovereign through the will of judges and the Judiciary.

The greatest blunder of advocates of a moral, fixed, biblical interpretation of the U.S. Constitution make is forgetting the source from which the legitimacy and authority for the U.S. Constitution is derived and abandoning the solid legal argument for a moral U.S. Constitution from that authoritative basis. Many history books *begin* with "We the People" and the Preamble, but ignore that this is a continuing hierarchy of ideas, legitimate authority, and documents necessarily dependent on each other.

"We the People" are the same people that are under legitimate government authority, granted unalienable rights from the Creator, which the Laws of Nature and of Nature's God entitle them, and the same people bound to a form of government that is consistent with Divine Law authority.

In fact, Madison, known as the "Father of the U.S. Constitution," argued to Congress that part of his original plan for the text of the U.S. Constitution included a "pre-Preamble"—the *same text* of the Declaration of Independence (penned by Jefferson) that claimed its only authority and legitimacy in Divine Law.

On June 8, 1789, Madison said to Congress:

> "First. That there be prefixed to the Constitution a declaration, that all power is originally vested in, and consequently derived from, the people. That Government is instituted and ought to be exercised for the benefit of the people; which consists in the enjoyment of life and liberty, with the right of acquiring and using property, and generally of pursuing and obtaining happiness and safety. That the people have an indubitable, unalienable, and indefeasible right to reform or change their Government, whenever it be found adverse or inadequate to the purposes of its institution."[100]

Ultimately, Congress deleted that addition from Madison as the text went through committees, and essentially determined that restating the Declaration of Independence was unnecessary—the Declaration of Independence had already given the U.S. Constitution its legitimacy and founding in Divine Law.[101]

Roger Sherman, a lawyer and member of the original five lawyers on the Declaration Committee, reasoned, "The truth is better asserted than it can be by any words what so ever. The words 'We the People' in the original U.S. Constitution are as copious and expressive as possible."[102]

Although a reiteration of the Declaration of Independence's own opening statements (the introduction and preamble) was not included in the final draft of the U.S. Constitution, the most critically important point is that the Founder lawyers themselves understood and acknowledged during this formation period that the Declaration of Independence (and its authority in Divine Law) was the legitimate legal basis upon which the U.S. Constitution is predicated.

It was unnecessary in the Founders' view to reiterate the Declaration of Independence's text within the U.S. Constitution's preamble because it was so objectively obvious a correlation and hierarchy.

We cannot concede the foundation of Constitutional interpretation and begin with the words of the Preamble, disconnecting the U.S. Constitution from its own legitimate authority as a form of government. The remainder of the Articles of the U.S. Constitution itself establish the form of government, in much the same way that the papers for closing of a real estate sale specify the terms of the already legitimately authoritative agreement and "reduce them to writing," which is the legal term of art to say that the document simply and precisely sets forth the terms.

The U.S. Constitution in this sense can appear to be like a contract if disconnected from the Declaration of Independence—the legal form is similar in that it simply sets out "the law" and what the Convention agreed upon for the best form of government (like a contract sets out the terms), but that does not mean that we can disregard why it exists and from where its authority and legitimacy are derived. It is not a contract in this sense whatsoever, nor did the Founders intend for it to be liberally interpreted as such.

We cannot begin the argument for a moral U.S. Constitution from the assumption that one interpretation is as equally valid as another, and it is up to man (acting through government) to simply agree on the best interpretation. The Founders specifically and purposefully designed this form of government so that the burden of proof is on the government to show how its authority is consistent with Divine Law and furthering the security of the people's unalienable rights.

If we concede the U.S. Constitution's grounding and do not hold firm that its only legitimate authority is vested in Divine Law, we have unknowingly acquiesced to the Social Contract Theory. Now, we have shifted the burden to ourselves to become the "moral majority" and prove why a simple majority of nine Supreme Court justices (a totalitarian form of government) should rule in accordance with biblical morality and principles.

This is the shrewd secular agenda that has slowly evolved into the prevalent social narrative, pushing a Social Contract Theory, and has eroded the true foundations of our nation, seeking to divorce the U.S. Constitution from its actual authority.

We will see examples of this cultural reconstruction in Chapter 10 and examine constitutional law opinions in light of Divine Law and the only legitimate basis for constitutional authority. But now that we understand the Founding Documents and the legal basis for a moral U.S. Constitution, we can look at the different theories of Constitutional interpretation and determine, based on the Divine Law authoritative standard, which theory is the only legitimate basis for Constitutional law and rational interpretation.

We see further within the text of the U.S. Constitution, that each Article and Amendment is consistent with Divine Law. Consider: if the Founders were beginning with a Social Contract Theory as the legal basis and authority, very likely at some point, if not many points, within the Founding Documents we would see evidence of a law or principle inconsistent with Divine Law that the Founder lawyers ratified.

Not only did the Founders specifically and textually refer to Divine Law and God as the "Creator" and "Supreme Judge" and numerous other examples, but we see that the final product did conform to a Divine Law standard and straddled that delicate balance between unalienable rights of the people and limited legitimate authority of civil government.

We see that the ratified form of the U.S. Constitution as a final product achieved a proper role of government, conforming to the Founders' three identified principles in the Declaration of Independence:

1. Government must secure the unalienable rights endowed by our Creator.
2. Government must not abridge these unalienable rights.
3. Government must exercise legitimate authority in securing and not abridging these rights, subject to "the laws of nature and of nature's God."

No government system predicated on the Social Contract Theory can claim this rational balance, and it would have been extremely unlikely that the Founders just happened to be so precisely faith-based and well-versed in biblical principles and then accidentally conformed a Social Contract Theory form of government entirely to Divine Law demands.

This important point must be underscored: Christians should not argue for an interpretation of the U.S. Constitution consistent with biblical principles simply because they believe in the biblical principles and are trying to "force" this morality in a social contract sense onto others, but rather, they should argue that the U.S. Constitution must be consistent with biblical principles because those principles *are also* consistent with Divine Law—the only rational legal basis of legitimate authority.

It does not matter to Divine Law whether an individual "agrees" with biblical principles—we are not free under Divine Law to negotiate the fixed, objective scientific and moral construct of law.

Certainly, the Founders acknowledged that any form of man-run civil government is necessarily imperfect in administration because man himself is imperfect, but all three constructs of law bearing on the text formed within the U.S. Constitution (the philosophical, statutory, and deference to scientific and moral law) are in accordance to the only legitimate role of government ordained by God through Divine Law.

This is no accident or incredible coincidence. This is by design and perfectly aligned with the legal knowledge and lawyerly understanding of the Founders.

John Adams, one of the most prominent practicing lawyers of this time in history wrote in a letter to Thomas Jefferson, "The general principles on which the fathers achieved independence ... were the general principles of Christianity. I will avow that I then believed, and now believe, that those general principles of Christianity are as eternal and immutable as the existence and attributes of God."[103]

The Bill of Rights

A brief commentary must be included specifically on the Bill of Right—what it is and what it is not. The Bill of Rights comprises the first ten Amendments to the U.S. Constitution, and all ten are important to consider as a whole.

As we have already seen in Hamilton's concerned admonishment, the Bill of Rights was not intended to *grant* rights to the people—our rights are given by God and are inalienable. The whole of the U.S.

Constitution, including the Bill of Rights, is to grant certain powers and specific limitations to the federal government from the people in order to preserve their rights.

While the U.S. Constitution granted specific limited powers to the federal government, the Bill of Rights provided specific limitations on federal government power. The text of each amendment is written to the government and places direct limitations on what the government cannot do.

For example, the text of the First Amendment reads:

> *Congress shall make no law respecting an establishment of religion, or prohibiting the free exercise thereof; or abridging the freedom of speech, or of the press; or the right of the people to peaceably assemble, and to petition the Government for a redress of grievances.*[104]

This is a specific limitation on Congressional power—not a granting of a right to the people. All this Amendment is saying is that Congress does not have authority (express or implied) by the U.S. Constitution to make any laws either that prohibit the free exercise of religion or that respect an establishment of religion.

The most common misunderstanding of the purpose of the Bill of Rights is that it exists to grant people their rights or tell them specifically what their rights are, or that the only rights of the people are those listed in the Bill of Rights. This is the exact opposite purpose and a complete misunderstanding. Taken with an understanding of the U.S. Constitution as a whole and that it exists to provide limited powers to the federal government, the Bill of Rights was included to expressly dictate specific limits to federal power on certain rights that the Founders believed were most important and could be most easily infringed upon by a too-powerful federal government.

As James Madison wrote in a letter to Thomas Jefferson,

"My own opinion has always been in favor of a bill of rights; provided it be so framed as not to imply powers not meant to be included in the enumeration. ... I have not viewed it in an important light—1. Because I conceive that in a certain degree...the rights in question are reserved by the manner in which the federal powers are granted. 2. Because there is great reason to fear that a positive declaration of some of the most essential rights could not be obtained in the requisite latitude. I am sure that the rights of conscience in particular, if submitted to public definition would be narrowed much more than they are likely ever to be by an assumed power."[105]

Understanding the true purpose of the Bill of Rights, it's incredibly important to also understand the purpose and scope of the Ninth and Tenth Amendments.

Ninth Amendment:

The enumeration in the Constitution, of certain rights, shall not be construed to deny or disparage others retained by the people.[106]

Tenth Amendment:

The powers not delegated to the United States by the Constitution, nor prohibited by it to the states, are reserved to the states respectively, or to the people.[107]

These two amendments were included as a compromise between Madison's view to include the Bill of Rights and Hamilton's view that it was unnecessary and dangerous. The text of the Ninth and Tenth Amendments together specifically address the concept of federalism: that the federal government exists in a very limited capacity to provide for the welfare of the several states and secure state sovereignty.

As the problem of federalism has increased, the so also has the problem of reconciling the two opposing powers: federal and state authority. The states were meant to largely govern themselves through their own legislatures, executive branches (governors), and judiciary. The idea of federalism is that whatever powers are not specifically granted to the federal government for the welfare of the whole union are specifically reserved for the states.

Yet we have seen a persistent erosion of state sovereignty as the federal government usurps more and more authority under misapplication and misconstruction of the text of the U.S. Constitution. The original concept of a limited federal government was to give *most* of the power to the states, and the federal government would operate only as necessary and proper for the good of the whole union.

This is the meaning of what is known as the General Welfare Clause[108] in the U.S. Constitution. "General" doesn't mean "anything" or whatever the federal government thinks it should have the power to legislate; it means only that which is necessary for the states generally and collectively. We can see how the federal government (all three branches) misconstrued and misapplied this clause to gain more power than is actually granted.

The overreaching of the federal government for especially the past 60 years, coupled with the increasing usurpation of the Supreme Court, has significantly contributed to the current constitutional crisis. Americans lack understanding in how our government is supposed to operate, because the federal government continues to overreach and tell us is has the power to do things it absolutely does not.

One of the recent examples is in the aftermath of the *Obergefell* decision and the general misunderstanding of the American population of the

Supreme Court's authority compared with laws already on the books at the state level.

We recall the Kentucky Court Clerk, Kim Davis, and her refusal to sign same-sex marriage licenses. This case was a clear example of two significant issues: federal usurpation of state sovereignty and a general misunderstanding of our system of government under the U.S. Constitution.

While the media largely portrayed the Kentucky issue as one of religious freedom versus equality, the actual issue was a Tenth Amendment issue. The Tenth Amendment has been almost obliterated from having any practical effect by the federal government in recent history for obvious reasons—conceding that the Tenth Amendment specifically limits federal powers would have the practical effect of actually limiting power that the federal government wants.

In the Kentucky case, the people of Kentucky had already passed an amendment to their state constitution in 2004 (by a 75 percent margin). This First Amendment to the Kentucky Constitution states:

> *Only a marriage between one man and one woman shall be valid or recognized as a marriage in Kentucky. A legal status identical or substantially similar to that of marriage for unmarried individuals shall not be valid or recognized.*[109]

This amendment is still good law, even after *Obergefell*. The U.S. Constitution is silent on domestic relations and does not provide any power to the federal government to regulate domestic relations issues, including marriage licensing. These issues have always been left to the states, and the power to issue marriage licensing comes from each state's own statutes. The Tenth Amendment is very clear that this is appropriate.

Obergefell was a significant usurpation and overreach of the federal government to attempt to regulate issues that are squarely in the jurisdiction of the states. Kim Davis was actually complying with Kentucky's state law (by which her own elected position as county clerk was created), which was not overridden or invalidated by *Obergefell*. Since June 2015, many states have been considering how to push back against this substantial usurpation.

The Supreme Court does not actually have the power to create law, and judicial review on the federal level extends only to those issues that are within federal jurisdiction. Domestic relations issues, including marriage licensing and the qualifications to obtain such license, have always properly been under the jurisdiction of each individual state.

This is such an important point to understand about the Bill of Rights. We will see in the next chapter how the Supreme Court has attempted to flip the Bill of Rights on its head and construe it as granting rights to the people that the government can then regulate, when in fact we have seen it is the exact opposite.

This misunderstanding and overreach of the federal government (via the Supreme Court) into the domain of marriage has created a huge problem that will not be easily straightened out. Overreaching of the federal government has been even further exacerbated and complicated by a confusion of the Supremacy Clause and the legal notion of "selective enforcement."

What is known as the "Supremacy Clause" in Article VI of the U.S. Constitution states:

> *This Constitution, and the laws of the United States which shall be made in pursuance thereof; and all treaties made, or which shall be made, under the authority of the United States, shall be the supreme law of the land; and the judges in every state shall be bound thereby, anything in the Constitution or laws of any State to the contrary notwithstanding.* [110]

The original meaning of the Supremacy Clause is consistent with the idea of federalism—when the states attempt to overreach into powers that are granted by the U.S. Constitution to the federal government, the federal government's law wins.

Importantly, this doesn't mean that whenever there is a conflict of law between states on issues that are within states' jurisdiction that the federal government should decide or has that power. There are numerous examples of states' laws differing from one another, which is entirely permissible under the U.S. Constitution.

For example, many states have a death penalty statute, and many other states do not. States are permitted to decide for themselves whether or not to have a death penalty statute. This doesn't mean for one second that someone living in a death penalty state does not have "equal protection" of laws under the Fourteenth Amendment. Yet in this example, we can see how the Supreme Court has completely taken the Equal Protection Clause out of context and applied it *selectively* to issues that they arbitrarily determine they want to control.

This is selective enforcement. The Supreme Court and federal government is deciding arbitrarily and selectively which issues they, in their sole discretion, constitute an impermissible breach of the Equal Protection Clause, and use that clause as a carte blanche justification to impose their decisions onto the states.

States have widely varying laws on numerous issues. States regulate licensing of many other types besides marriage: driver's licenses, professional licenses, etc. Just because a Colorado resident with a Colorado driver's license drives a vehicle on the roads in Texas does not mean that the Supreme Court now has jurisdiction over that license under "equal protection." Even if the Colorado driver receives a ticket in Texas, Colorado still has full and final jurisdiction over the Colorado driver's license (whether to revoke it or allow the driver to keep it). Texas has jurisdiction over the ticket received, but not the license.

The license allows the Colorado driver lawful access to the roads of Texas as a visiting driver, but under each state's law, a driver must pass the requirements and gain that state's driver's license upon establishing residency in that state within a certain period. The Colorado driver could not continue to drive in Texas after establishing residency in Texas and presume that her Colorado license is sufficient for Texas, under a "full faith and credit" theory.

There are numerous examples of this—virtually all licensing that is issued under the authority of a state agency and regulated by a state may be accepted or denied when the license holder transfers to a new state. New state; new state's licensing rules apply. This is true for everything from a cosmetology license to an attorney's bar license.

But the progressive agenda has carefully crafted the narrative to completely misconstrue the Equal Protection Clause (and to a lesser degree a "full faith and credit" argument) to confer federal authority outside the bounds of legitimate constitutional conferral, thereby attempting to settle state jurisdiction issues through a usurpation of federal authority.

If we go back and look at the original text of the Supremacy Clause, Article IV does not contain a blanket assertion of federalism over every state law or every subject matter. It is textually contained to:

1. "This Constitution, and the laws of the United States which shall be made in pursuance thereof"—The limited powers specifically granted to the federal government through the Constitution; and
2. "All treaties made, or which shall be made, under the authority of the United States"—Any foreign treaties that the national federal government (rather than the individual states) would naturally negotiate on behalf of the union.

Some legal scholars and the current majority of the Supreme Court argues that the Supremacy Clause is a blanket presumption that wherever there is a conflict of laws between a state and the federal government, then the federal government wins as supreme law of the land. This is an incorrect and illogical assertion when reading the entirety of the U.S. Constitution together as a whole and seeing that the specific intent of the U.S. Constitution was to grant specific limited powers to the federal government and reserve all other powers to the states.

Further, it would be nonsensical for the Founders to believe it necessary to include the second category of treaties if the meaning of the Supremacy Clause were intended to include literally every conflict between the federal government and state laws.

Justice Roberts wisely commented on this incredible overreach in his dissent in *Obergefell*, writing:

> "Nowhere is the majority's extravagant conception of judicial supremacy more evident than in its description—and dismissal—of the public debate regarding same-sex marriage. ... The truth is that today's decision rests on nothing more than the majority's own conviction that same-sex couples should be allowed to marry because they want to... Whatever force that belief may have as a matter of moral philosophy, it has no more basis in the Constitution... The Constitution itself says nothing about marriage, and the Framers [through the Ninth and Tenth Amendment] thereby entrusted the States with '[t]he whole subject of the domestic relations of husband and wife.'"[111]

We have to understand what the Bill of Rights actually does functionally within the federal government and for the states, and reclaim the state sovereignty inherent in the Ninth and Tenth Amendment. But first, we will look at the recent history of the Supreme Court's usurpation and how we arrived at this constitutional crisis.

CHAPTER 9

THEORIES OF CONSTITUTIONAL LAW: JUDICIAL RESTRAINT VS. JUDICIAL ACTIVISM

"One of the beautiful boasts of our municipal jurisprudence is that Christianity is a part of the Common Law. There never has been a period at which the Common Law did not recognize Christianity as lying at its foundations."[112]

- Supreme Court Justice Joseph Story

When we use the term "constitutional law," lawyers are referring to the body of legal opinions interpreting the written text of the U.S. Constitution and forming judicial opinions, case law, and precedent within the statutory construct of law.

As was stated at the outset, there is a substantial difference between "Constitutional interpretation" as a foundational analysis of just the text of the U.S. Constitution and its foundational roots and "Constitutional Law" as the history after the U.S. Constitution, which accepts as correct and incorporating the 225 years of Supreme Court opinions on the U.S. Constitution.

Put into a chart, we can see the obvious distinction in definitions:

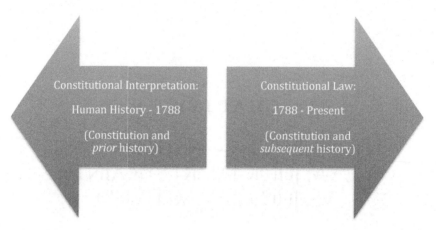

Constitutional Interpretation vs. Constitutional Law Arrows

Lawyers have broadly categorized two different theories of Constitutional Law (meaning the U.S. Constitution and subsequent Supreme Court opinions and case law): Judicial Activism and Judicial Restraint.

Judicial Activism is the theory that interpretation of the U.S. Constitution and rulings on constitutional law are based on current social opinion, political considerations, and a fluid, subjective meaning to the text of the U.S. Constitution itself.

Judicial Restraint is the theory that interpretation of the U.S. Constitution and rulings on constitutional law are based on *limited* judicial power, and a fixed, objective interpretation, consistent with the Founders' original intent and subject to legitimate authority.

Through these definitions and our initial question regarding the problem of morality in secular government, we can readily see that Judicial Activism is borne out of secular humanism and the Social Contract Theory, and that Judicial Restraint is consistent with Divine Law. Because the *Marbury* decision gave the Supreme Court the province of judicial review, the Judiciary still had to practically and pragmatically apply this doctrine within the judicial framework.

We will see as we go through important case holdings in American history how the Supreme Court's initial exercise of Judicial Restraint began to evolve into Judicial Activism.

This evolution occurred due to two key shifts: first, the cultural shift and new perception of the Social Contract Theory as the basis of authority for the U.S. Constitution and the law itself; and second, the Court's realization of its actual power through judicial review and subversive desire of members on the Court to substitute their own judgment as Sovereign in lieu of Divine Law and the U.S. Constitution's actual authority.

Importantly, the concept and philosophy of judicial review does not inherently mean that the Supreme Court has authority *over* the U.S. Constitution or to read into it authority to practice Judicial Activism. Judicial review, when exercised in the limited scope and capacity that the John Marshall Supreme Court originally envisioned, can function in accordance with the separation of powers and clear delineation of the U.S. Constitution's mandate to the Judiciary without overstepping that limited agency authority. The U.S. Constitution itself should still serve to be a check and full-stop limitation on the Supreme Court's authority and exercise of judicial review.

Consider the foundational differences and the ultimate top-level conclusion of the basis of Supreme Court U.S. Constitutional interpretation in these two hierarchy structures:

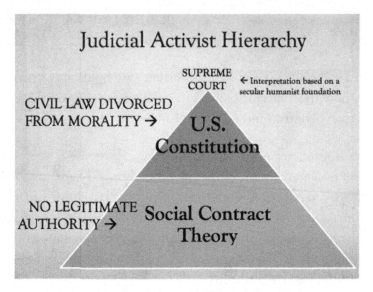

Judicial Activist Hierarchy

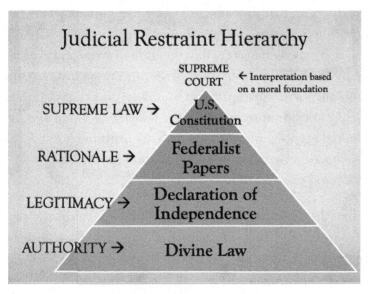

Judicial Restraint Hierarchy

After *Marbury* and the concept of judicial review was in place, the Supreme Court still originally exercised Judicial Restraint and, as Justice Story observed, still recognized and even "boasted" that

Christian principles were always a part of American jurisprudence and at the foundation of the common law (another term for the statutory construct).

But as secular humanism and the Social Contract Theory began to control the societal narrative, jurisprudence and the Supreme Court also began to ignore our foundational authority in Divine Law.

One of the critical decisions in Supreme Court case law history that further usurped legitimate Constitutional authority was the 1965 opinion, *Griswold v. Connecticut*.[113]

Justice William Douglas delivered the majority opinion that declared a new facet of the U.S. Constitution: a vast "penumbra" within the U.S. Constitution's text. While *penumbra* has since become a legal term of art with its own legal definition, the original term finds its roots in physical science: "A space of partial illumination between the perfect shadow ... on all sides and the full light."[114]

Borrowing this scientific term, the *Griswold* Court applied the idea of indistinct or non-expressed terms and rights within the "space" between Constitutional text. This was quite literally reading between the lines.

The majority opinion stated that the specific, textual guarantees in the Bill of Rights have these "penumbras" that are "formed by emanations from those guarantees that help give them life and substance."[115]

In other words, the Court creatively redefined the directly stated limitation in the U.S. Constitution on the authority of the federal government, which was specifically included at the very end of the original Bill of Rights in the Tenth Amendment: "The powers not delegated to the United States by the U.S. Constitution, nor prohibited by it to the states, are reserved to the states respectively, or to the people."[116]

Hamilton's fear in including a Bill of Rights in the U.S. Constitution was grimly realized—the federal government Sovereign artfully usurped unjust power that was *not* granted by the U.S. Constitution and, through the *Griswold* decision, extended federal government power specifically textually prohibited by the Tenth Amendment.

And it was even worse than Hamilton predicted.

Remember, the Bill of Rights was included not to confer rights from the government to the people (the Declaration of Independence recognized that these rights are endowed by God our Creator), but rather to limit the federal government's authority on specific rights, and to reserve civil government's limited authority to secure those rights to the state level. Redefining the U.S. Constitution's clear, precise intent to limit federal powers into a murky, shadowy penumbra effectively unlocked federal power to a nearly unlimited capacity.

Because this so-called "penumbra" is in the grey, indistinct area between the lines of the U.S. Constitution, the Judicial Sovereign can now read into it anything it "sees" and there is no super-Supreme Court or other source of accountability to assess what the justices declare that they see.

This state of affairs is reminiscent of the Hans Christian Andersen story, "The Emperor's New Clothes." In this tale, the Emperor convinces his subjects about his new suit of clothes, invisible to those who are unfit or too stupid to see their beauty. When the Emperor parades his "new clothes" in front of his subjects, no one can see them, but they all fear saying so because they do not want to be perceived as stupid or unfit, as everyone *else* must see the clothes.

But then a child speaks the truth and says, "But he hasn't got any clothes on!"[117]

Do we really believe that a Supreme Court can, by mere virtue of its lofty position, see into these dark crevices of the U.S. Constitution that others unfit or too stupid cannot see?

No. The Supreme Court hasn't got any clothes on!

Yet the Sovereign boldly asserted this new penumbra doctrine, and it is now taught as a central portion of Constitutional Law in all American law schools. New generations of lawyers are raised to believe in the validity of this absurdity and practice law according to this accepted doctrine.

But what is not taught in Constitutional Law courses is the appeal to legitimate authority that we saw in the text of the Declaration of Independence, Federalist Papers, and the U.S. Constitution itself— that the Founder lawyers intended to create a form of government whose sole legitimate role is securing the unalienable rights of the people, not becoming their Sovereign.

Recall the five principles of Originalism in Chapter 5. Once we add a "penumbra" to the U.S. Constitution, we have added invisible "text" that the author did not intend and did not mean and we are replacing genuine meaning with literal absurdity.

Yet the Social Contract Theory and Judicial Activism has taken hold, and case law outflowing from *Griswold* only further usurped Constitutional authority to empower this growing judicial Sovereign. Now, this vast penumbra has provided a clever way for the Supreme Court to read into the U.S. Constitution literally anything it wants to decide and whatever way it wants to decide it.

Incredibly, this is backward to the U.S. Constitution in two ways.

First, the original purpose of the Bill of Rights was to specifically limit the government's decision-making power on unalienable rights that are universally held by the people. The list of rights

Jenna Ellis, Esq.

was not comprehensive, but the Tenth Amendment granted the remaining rights *not* specifically discussed to the providence of the state government to secure. The Judicial Activist view has allowed the Judiciary to take away these rights from the people and then decide how and when and in what form it will choose to give them back to the people.

Second, the government is using this invention of a penumbra to substitute its own value judgment on which rights are fundamental and what weight should be given to certain rights and in what proportion to other rights—*entirely* misconstruing the U.S. Constitution's clear restriction of government authority and absolute reservation of unalienable rights to the people, as endowed by their Creator through Divine Law.

This is the natural consequence and conclusion of the Social Contract Theory's application. Once we the people unwittingly allowed the Sovereign's substituted judgment in determining what ideals and morals *it* values more, we receded further into murky depths of the secular humanist swamp.

A recent decision by a Canadian appellate court predicts the gloomy future of the next natural consequence of Judicial Activism through secular humanism for the United States. Canada is only a few decades ahead of the United States in its continued embrace and application of the Social Contract Theory's ultimate conclusion about rights and freedoms.

This 2015 opinion not only decided a case against the unalienable right to freedom of religion because it was outweighed by the "greater good" of protecting a reinvented definition of equality, but the opinion also clearly but incorrectly stated that a judicial court has authority to make such a value judgment at all. This subjective value equity test is alarming and an obvious usurpation of government authority. In its opinion, which specifically stated its authority to resolve the issue in a Rousseau-like duty to "public interest," the Ontario Superior Court held:

> "[W]e observe that the area of human rights is one that continues to **evolve**. The attitudes of the general population towards such issues **change** almost daily. Certainly those attitudes … have changed considerably in the last fifteen years. As such, this area of law is probably the most **fluid** of any area of law in terms of the appropriate application of legal principles and the context in which they come to be applied. Some of the presumptions or predispositions that **may have existed in the past, and which may have informed decisions at that time, cannot now be safely relied upon** for the continuation of attitudes that were previously enunciated"[118] (emphasis added).

This is Judicial Activism at its most threatening to the very foundation of legitimate legal authority. Notice the fluid and subjective terms that the Court uses: "evolve," "attitudes of the general population … change almost daily," and "fluid" area of law. American jurisprudence continues to follow this primrose path and cede more and more powers to the dark ambiguity of Judicial Activism and a Supreme Court Sovereign.

Even more startling in the supposedly legitimate existence in *Griswold* of the U.S. Constitution's penumbra is the acceptance and enthusiasm the general public has for this incredible justification of Judicial Activism and blatant substitution of the Court's majority's best judgment for the *rights* of the people.

But the Emperor hasn't got any clothes on!

A quotation attributed to Adolf Hitler states, "The best way to take control over a people and control them utterly is to take a little of their freedom at a time, to erode rights by a thousand tiny and almost imperceptible reductions. In this way the people will not see those rights and freedoms being removed until past the point at which these changes cannot be reversed."[119]

The U.S. Constitution is *not* fluid, *not* filled with shadowed legal inferences that can only be observed by the wise, infallible Sovereign.

All of the evidence in America's Founding Documents—direct, circumstantial, textual, relevant, and contemporaneous—is consistent with Divine Law as the legal basis for the U.S. Constitution, and further, is the only source of legitimate authority.

We have seen the Founders' framework as lawyers, defined what the law is and the logical hierarchy and interrelationship of the Founding Documents, the rational consistency of Divine Law and inherent absurdity of Divine Law, and reviewed the text of the Founding Documents themselves to directly discern the plain meaning of the text. Finally, if that is not enough, one additional legal argument for Divine Law as the only rational, authoritative basis exists:

The burden of proof.

When evaluating this debate, we often approach the table at either an equal position with secular humanists and social contract theorists or, even worse, allow them to shift the burden of proof and we start in the losing position. In shifting the burden, we allow the secular position of fluidity, penumbra, and no fixed, objective meaning to be the default conclusion for Constitutional interpretation and it becomes *our* problem and *our* burden to prove to a reasonable certainty why there is a legal basis for a biblical and moral interpretation of the U.S. Constitution and argue for Judicial Restraint.

Secular humanist theorists almost always assume that the U.S. Constitution is a fluid document unless proven otherwise, and usually only in very specific instances, of which the number of instances is rapidly shrinking.

Incredibly, we have incontrovertible evidence that the Founding Documents derived their legitimate authority in Divine Law, yet we have still allowed the burden to slowly shift as the secular humanist agenda begins eroding this authoritative basis and the misconception of an American Social Contract Theory has taken hold of the basic viewpoint of the general population.

Here are two key reasons why this shift is impermissible and unreasonable, from an objectively logical standpoint:

1. *We do know the Founders' intent and the objective meaning of the U.S. Constitution.*

   Secular theorists argue that we cannot actually know the Founders' intent, and we have to look at the penumbra of the U.S. Constitution to conjure the unclear, fluid meaning. But we have the best evidence—the original Founding Documents themselves. There is no conjecture about what is or is not contained in the actual physical text of the Declaration of Independence or the U.S. Constitution. We are not speculating what the original U.S. Constitution "may" have looked like because the document itself was lost or destroyed or we only have copies.

   In a legal case, the best evidence is the original document itself and established legal theory and principles tell us that we only look outside the "four corners" of the document (another legal term of art meaning "the plainly understood meaning of just the written text itself—the 'four corners' of the paper") if there is a dispute in the contract's *formation.*

   For example, consider a claim that the term "magenta" in a written contract was understood by one party to mean "pink" and the other party to mean "purple." Both parties agreed upon the term "magenta," but with significantly different understandings. Importantly, though, the term "magenta" appearing in the document itself is not disputed.

We don't look outside the four corners just because we don't like what it plainly says *after* we already agreed to it and we want to create a penumbra and find hidden meanings.

In our example, if the document term was "magenta" and had a plain meaning that both parties understood to mean a specific shade of pink, one party could not go back and ask the Court to read into the document "pink...and also any other color in the shadows of the spectrum" or substitute the term "blue" instead of "magenta" because it now suits that party's interest better.

Courts also take into account the sophistication of the person or people who wrote the legal document or agreed to the terms. A non-lawyer may not know the plain meaning of a legal term of art more complicated than our "magenta" example, but courts presume that educated attorneys know the law and the plain meaning of the legal terms.

Similarly, the U.S. Constitution as a legal document has a plain meaning and was specifically ratified as the complete document by the sophisticated lawyers that drafted it. There is no legal reason to look beyond the plain text of the U.S. Constitution or read into it something that is not clearly there, including a "vast penumbra."

These well-established and generally accepted legal doctrines go back well before American jurisprudence as the most fair, logical, and rational way to read a document and interpret what it says. No Court will ever ask, "well what about the penumbra?"

Yet our Judiciary is trying to sell us on the idea that somehow this *one* document should be read entirely differently then the rest of the legal documents establishing law or rules throughout the history of contract law jurisprudence.

2. *No contemporaneous documents from the Founder lawyers suggest a Social Contract Theory or amoral interpretation.*

All of the best evidence we have—the original Founding Documents and other letters and secondary sources of rationale from the Founders—points directly, specifically, and unambiguously to self-evident, objective, God-given, moral, fixed, Divine Law foundations.

Rousseau was actually a contemporary of the Founding Fathers, completing his work *The Social Contract* in France in 1762. This political framework and ideology was spreading across Europe during the Enlightenment period, and yet the Declaration of Independence and the U.S. Constitution never *once* referred to anything that could even possibly be construed to be a Social Contract Theory.

One of two logical outcomes for this circumstance is possible: either the Founders rejected the Social Contract Theory as an illegitimate basis of authority and chose instead to specifically refer to self-evident truths on the basis of nature's God and our Creator, or, the Founders did not read Rousseau's work and the Social Contract Theory was not even within their known wheelhouse of options to discuss as a Constitutional basis.

Either way, Divine Law foundations are unambiguously present as the foundation.

Further, as we saw in the text of the Declaration of Independence itself, the Founder lawyers referred to "the

Laws of Nature and of nature's God." Only *later* did Supreme Court cases begin to opine about the penumbra and apply the Social Contract Theory—completely ignoring the true legal basis of the U.S. Constitution.

When looking at the intent of an individual's actions, we can only apply the information that was contemporaneous to that conduct.

For example, if a man decided to go to the grocery store and upon his arrival, found his neighbor was also there, it would not be logical proof to say that he went to the store *with the intent* to meet his neighbor. He did not possess that information until after he made his decision to go to the grocery store. In the same way, we cannot base a legitimate interpretation of the U.S. Constitution reading documents that comment on the intent of U.S. Constitution after it was written.

We actually use this same logic when applied to the history of who the Founding Fathers were and who was physically present at the Constitutional Convention. We have records written contemporaneously with this actual event that record its history, from eyewitnesses who were in a position of knowing who was in attendance.

Imagine if another document claiming to be an additional Federalist Paper was written 200 years after the Constitutional Convention when everyone who possibly could have been an eyewitness would no longer be living, and this paper claimed that Barack Obama was present at the Constitutional Convention.

We would readily discern the absurdity of this idea for several reasons: First, the actual physical impossibility of Barack Obama being present in 1787 when he was born in 1961;

and second, in all of the writings and historical documents, nowhere ever was there any recording of Barack Obama present in contemporaneous documents. So we would realize the author of this document had no personal knowledge of who was and was not present, unlike the authors who were eyewitnesses.

In this sense, it does not matter if one eyewitness author mentions a speech by Benjamin Franklin and does not record that John Adams was also there, and another eyewitness does record that John Adams was there, perhaps because this eyewitness had a personal conversation with John Adams. Perspectives can change, depending on what is most important to the author or the purpose of the eyewitness account.

The point is that none of the contemporaneous authors and none of the Founders ever suggested that the U.S. Constitution and Declaration of Independence were founded upon anything except the Judeo-Christian worldview, rooted in Divine Law, which was contemporaneously clearly stated. Repeatedly.

Only through the lapse of time has the U.S. Constitution been interpreted to be a "living" document—at the time of the writing of the Founding Documents, it was known to be a complete, fixed, plainly meaningful document.

Our primary sources for Constitutional interpretation all come from the latter half of 18th century: The Declaration of Independence, the Federalist Papers, personal letters and other contemporaneous documents from the Founding Fathers, and the U.S. Constitution itself. By contrast, the *Griswold* opinion containing the assertion of a "penumbra" was written nearly 200 years later in 1965.

As John Adams wrote, "How strangely will the tools of a Tyrant pervert the plain meaning of words!"[120]

CHAPTER 10

CONSTITUTIONAL LAW CASE STUDIES: A SYSTEMATIC REPLACEMENT OF DIVINE LAW WITH SOCIAL CONTRACT THEORY

"Governments could not give the rights essential to happiness… We claim them from a higher source: from the King of kings, and Lord of all the Earth. They are not annexed to us by parchments and seals. They are created in us by the decrees of Providence."[121]

- General John Dickinson,
Signatory of the U.S. Constitution

How did we actually get from the ratification in 1788 and the plain, fixed meaning of the U.S. Constitution, founded in Divine Law and objective morality and rooted in the Declaration of Independence, to the secular Sovereign of the Supreme Court freely reinterpreting the text and conforming it to their own will?

Let's analyze the key Constitutional Law shifts in textual analysis after *Marbury* (the case that established judicial review) and gain a broader perspective of what was shifting in the nation's "common sense."

Remember, the opinions of the Supreme Court that comprise our American Constitutional Law are not the text of the U.S. Constitution itself, but an interpretation of that text. Though these Supreme Court rulings are operating today as controlling precedent because of the doctrine of judicial review, this does not necessarily mean that the opinions of the Court are decisively accurate interpretations.

Recall what Justice Jackson said about the Supreme Court: "Reversal by a higher court is not proof that justice is thereby better done. There is no doubt that if there were a super-Supreme Court, a substantial proportion of our reversals of state courts would also be reversed. We are not final because we are infallible, but we are infallible only because we are final."[122]

As we discuss the more recent history of Constitutional Law, consider how the foundation and legal basis in Divine Law versus the Social Contract Theory has changed the outcome of the top-level critical moral issues: abortion, marriage, privacy, education, "separation of church and state," the role of government, and many more *moral* concerns.

Fourteenth Amendment, 1868

To understand how the Supreme Court has deftly taken liberties with the text of the U.S. Constitution, we must begin with the ratification of the Fourteenth Amendment in 1868, because this is one of the primary texts that the Court frequently cites to as its authority for decisions like *Obergefell*. It remains one of the most highly litigated sections of the U.S. Constitution—specifically, its Due Process Clause and its Equal Protection Clause.

The historical context of the Fourteenth Amendment is critical to understanding the text, just as we saw with the text of the

Declaration of Independence and the original U.S. Constitution. The Fourteenth Amendment was deliberated and included as one of the Reconstruction Amendments following the Civil War.

Obviously, the Fourteenth Amendment was ratified nearly 100 years after the U.S. Constitution was originally ratified. The U.S. Constitution sets forth the procedure for amendments in Article V:

> "The Congress, whenever two thirds of both houses shall deem it necessary, shall propose amendments to this U.S. Constitution, or, on the application of the legislatures of two thirds of the several states, shall call a convention for proposing amendments, which, in either case, shall be valid to all intents and purposes, as part of this U.S. Constitution, when ratified by the legislatures of three fourths of the several states, or by conventions in three fourths thereof, as the one or the other mode of ratification may be proposed by the Congress; provided that no amendment which may be made prior to the year one thousand eight hundred and eight shall in any manner affect the first and fourth clauses in the ninth section of the first article; and that no state, without its consent, shall be deprived of its equal suffrage in the Senate."[123]

The Founders recognized that additions to the U.S. Constitution might be necessary, as government is not infallible. They did make the process incredibly difficult so that the U.S. Constitution could not easily change, but only when a sufficient majority of Congress *or* the states determined it necessarily. Consider how much more difficult this process is than merely one case decided among nine Supreme Court Justices.

Importantly, the Founders never provided a mechanism to completely overhaul the role and scope of government clearly delineated from the Declaration of Independence. As they recognized at the outset of the Constitutional Convention, the form of government may take various and equally valid shapes—there is not only one form consistent with Divine Law. But whatever form we do have, that form must be in conformance with Divine Law.

Interestingly, our Judiciary frequently asks the question, *Is it Constitutional?,* when we should be asking that question, but also, *Is it Declarational? Is it in conformance with Divine Law and the proper role of government—that is, to secure our God-given rights?*

Simply because a formal process to ratify an amendment to the U.S. Constitution exists does not mean that the other foundational legal document and the nation's foundation in legitimate authority of Divine Law allows ratification of amendments that are antithetical to the proper role of government. Remember, this was the very complaint that the Founders made against England—that the English government, through their king and Parliament, had usurped the only proper role of government.

Government is and always must still be *under* its source of authority, and the U.S. Constitution must still always be in conformance with the outlined declaration (in the Declaration of Independence) of the role of government—to secure our God-given rights. The process of amending the U.S. Constitution simply provides a mechanism to tailor the U.S. Constitution to the form of government best suited to fulfill its legitimate role and purpose.

So the Fourteenth Amendment and its interpretation must be viewed from an historical contextual standpoint, and also from a lens consistent with the proper role and scope of government.

Historically, the purpose and scope of the Fourteenth Amendment was to grant African Americans citizenship and equal civil and legal rights, in conjunction with the Thirteenth Amendment and the Fifteenth Amendment. The Fourteenth Amendment was the final product of several separate proposals that began in 1866. Congress found adoption of these three amendments necessary under Article V because the United States needed to address former slaves and those emancipated during the Civil War.

Because the Fourteenth Amendment contains a Due Process Clause and an Equal Protection Clause, this Amendment has been the basis for relatively modern Supreme Court decisions seeking to reinterpret its historical meaning and creatively "find" a text in the U.S. Constitution to support Social Contract Theory conclusions.

The Fifth Amendment to the U.S. Constitution (which was also one of the original amendments contained within the Bill of Rights), also includes a Due Process Clause (differing substantially in legal terms from the clause in the Fourteenth Amendment not within the scope of our discussion here), but it was not until 1954 and the decision in *Bolling v. Sharpe* that the Court reverse-incorporated equal protection into the Fifth Amendment.

The *Bolling* Court held that "[T]he concepts of equal protection and due process, both stemming from our American ideal of fairness, are not mutually exclusive."[124]

This opinion presents a very critical problem: This is a *moral* judgment, citing to an "American ideal" or value rather than any concrete text or legitimate authority within the U.S. Constitution or its foundations, and so the Sovereign Court is usurping its role and imposing its own morality for Divine Law.

Further, this idea of reverse incorporation means that the Court was literally adding to the text of the Fifth Amendment unilaterally and outside the scope of the Judicial Branch's authority. (Remember, Article V delineates a clear process that must be followed to actually amend the U.S. Constitution.)

Like taking one verse of the Bible out of context and building an entire doctrine around it, the Supreme Court has transmogrified the Fourteenth Amendment.

This is known as the "Incorporation Doctrine"—the idea that the Supreme Court can "incorporate" into the U.S. Constitution's text anything it deems necessary to interpret the U.S. Constitution. By calling it a doctrine, the Court pretends it is something other than exactly what it is—complete legal fiction.

This doctrine gained momentum in the 1940s – 1960s and operates to use the Due Process and Equal Protection Clauses in the Fourteenth Amendment to define new fundamental "rights" antithetical to Divine Law morals and assert federal power to regulate these rights, when such regulatory power is not explicitly granted in the U.S. Constitution's text because the so-called right is nonexistent.

As we will see, starting in the 1940s, this doctrine increased its academic traction among the Supreme Court and legal scholars, and it continues to operate to impose the Sovereign's moral value judgments and literally read anything into the U.S. Constitution.

Everson v. Board of Education, 1947

Prior to 1947, the First Amendment text, "Congress shall make no law respecting an establishment of religion"[125] functioned essentially how the Bill of Rights was originally intended to—imposing limits on the federal government's regulating of these fundamental rights, thus operating to secure the inalienable right of the people to practice their faith and sincerely held religious beliefs.

Importantly, this was never construed to mean that any overlap between government action and religious beliefs (such as prayer in public school or on the Congress floor, or the Ten Commandments being displayed on government property, etc.) was unconstitutional.

In fact, the universally understood common sense was that Divine Law's authority is above government and gives government its only role and legitimacy. It was commonly understood that biblical principles, God as Divine Lawgiver, and basic morality were a part of society and government.

Everson v. Board of Education[126] changed that paradigm entirely and redesigned a completely new interpretation of Constitutional text, which itself was unconstitutional.

Socially, the world was shifting from a common understanding of the "Laws of Nature and of Nature's God" that the Founders presumed to be ordinarily understood to the secular premises of the "free man" and the Social Contract Theory espoused by Jean-Paul Sartre (from *Nausea*, published in 1938, to *The Age of Reason*, published in 1945, to dozens of other works published through 1947 and beyond), building upon the earlier writings of Rousseau.

Prominent feminist and social theorist Simone de Beauvior also published her first novel *She Came to Stay* in 1943. This work was a fictionalized version of her and Sartre's open sexual relationship and lauded a new era of open sexuality, feminist sexual equality, polyamory, and sexual acts free from traditional restraints. De Beauvior also published discussions of secular existential ethics beginning in 1947.

In *The Second Sex*, de Beauvior argues that traditional morality is merely a social construct and that women are as capable of free choice as men—a female is not born a woman (or a "lesser" sex), but becomes one through her submission to a Paternalistic social construct.[127]

The common sense of universal morality was not so common anymore. The open embrace of the Sexual Revolution was completely inconsistent with Divine Law morality. As a consequence, in order to "liberate" ourselves from the commonly understood restraints of moral law, our civil law had to begin to reflect a morality other than Divine Law.

The term "Sexual Revolution," means and includes the paradigm changes in attitudes, social activism, and open embrace of the secular humanist philosophy starting in the 1920s and fully developing openly in the 1960s that man is the origin of all rights and there is no such thing as objective morality.

With the rise of feminism and the women's rights movement, there was a dynamic and pervasive cultural shift in sexual practices and attitudes about sexuality apart from traditional morality and social norms. Sex outside the bounds of traditional heterosexual marriage, in any form, with any partner(s), and for any reason, was becoming more socially acceptable and de-stigmatized. Sex was beginning to be pleasure- and individually-focused rather than moral- and procreation-focused.

The natural consequences of increased sexual activity (childbirth—a good thing within the bounds of traditional marriage—and sexually transmitted diseases) were undesirable. Under the guise of "women's rights," birth control, abortions, and unplanned pregnancy alternatives to motherhood became the pragmatic response.

By the 1960s, Margaret Sanger, President Lyndon B. Johnson, Planned Parenthood, the National Organization of Women, and even the FDA became open advocates for "women's rights," or more truthfully stated, advocates for the Sexual Revolution and making sex outside traditional heterosexual marriage socially acceptable.

The main premise asserted by the Women's Rights Movement, as an outflow of the Sexual Revolution, was the complete destruction of the culture. As one author concisely stated, the Women's Right's Movement thesis was Marxist philosophy:

> "The family is a den of slavery with the man as the Bourgeoisie and the woman and children as the Proletariat. The only hope for the women's 'liberation' (communism's favorite word for leading minions into inextricable slavery; 'liberation,' and much like 'collective'—please run from it, run for your life) was this new 'Women's Movement.' Her [Kate Millett's] books captivated the academic classes and soon 'Women's Studies' courses were installed in colleges in a steady wave across the nation with Kate Millett books as required reading. ... By the time Women's Studies professors finish with your daughter, she will be a shell of the innocent girl you knew, who's soon convinced that although she should be flopping down with every boy she fancies, she should not, by any means, get pregnant. And so, as a practitioner of promiscuity, she becomes a wizard of prevention techniques, especially abortion. The goal of Women's Liberation is to wear each female down to losing all empathy for boys, men or babies."[128]

Marxist theory is rooted in Communism, and these socialist values have effectively run two parallel threads to take over the culture and effectively promote Communism through the Courts. In a list of current communist goals, Dr. Cleon Skousen provides specific examples revealed in *The Naked Communist*, written in 1958 and read into the Congressional Record in 1963. Here are a few items from the list:

> #16. Use technical decisions of the courts to weaken basic American institutions by claiming their activities violate civil rights.

#25. Break down cultural standards of morality by promoting pornography and obscenity in books, magazines, motion pictures, radio, and TV.

#26. Present homosexuality, degeneracy and promiscuity as "normal, natural, healthy."

#27. Infiltrate the churches and replace revealed religion with "social" religion. Discredit the Bible and emphasize the need for intellectual maturity which does not need a "religious crutch."

#28. Eliminate prayer or any phase of religious expression in the schools on the ground that it violates the principle of "separation of church and state."

#29. Discredit the American Constitution by calling it inadequate, old-fashioned, out of step with modern needs, a hindrance to cooperation between nations on a worldwide basis.

#30-33. Discredit the American Founding Fathers. Eliminate all laws or procedures which interfere with the operation of the Communist apparatus.

#40. Discredit the family as an institution. Encourage promiscuity and easy divorce. [129]

This dangerous social shift was beginning to show in the rationale of Supreme Court decisions as early as the 1940s that embraced the Social Contract Theory and secular humanism, reflecting the current trends rather than remaining consistent to the original U.S. Constitutional text.

In the landmark *Everson* decision, the U.S. Supreme Court decontextualized the First Amendment's Establishment Clause and redefined it in terms of a "wall of separation of church and state" for the first time. Objective morality and basic religious doctrine (i.e. Divine Law), of course insisted that sex outside of traditional heterosexual marriage is immoral.

So the first step was to separate Divine Law morality from the civil law—especially in public schools. Take out of public schools any education that involves God or morality, teach them "sex education" early, and by the time they get to college, they will be ripe for following the Sexual Revolution and their own Rousseau-influenced "independence," devoid of morality.

The *Everson* majority stated,

> "The 'establishment of religion' clause of the First Amendment means at least this: Neither a state nor the Federal Government can set up a church. Neither can pass laws which aid one religion, aid all religions or prefer one religion over another. Neither can force nor influence a person to go to or to remain away from church against his will or force him to profess a belief or disbelief in any religion. No person can be punished for entertaining or professing religious beliefs or disbeliefs, for church attendance or non-attendance. No tax in any amount, large or small, can be levied to support any religious activities or institutions, whatever they may be called, or whatever form they may adopt to teach or practice religion. Neither a state nor the Federal Government can, openly or secretly, participate in the affairs of any religious organizations or groups and vice versa. In the words of Jefferson, the clause against establishment of religion by law was intended to erect 'a wall of separation between Church and State.'"[130]

Jefferson's words come from a letter to the Danbury Baptist Church. Again, context is critically important. Though the notion of "separation of church and state" is found nowhere within the text of the U.S. Constitution or the legally operative Founding Documents, we might be tempted to argue that Jefferson's phrase (and *Everson's* particular definition) should be included in the rationale of the U.S. Constitution, like the Federalist Papers and other contemporaneous writings.

Indeed, we should take this contemporaneous writing into account, but the *whole* writing and *in context*. This is the full text of the letter, as documented by the Library of Congress, sent in 1802:

> "To messers. Nehemiah Dodge, Ephraim Robbins, & Stephen S. Nelson, a committee of the Danbury Baptist association in the state of Connecticut.
>
> Gentlemen
>
> The affectionate sentiments of esteem and approbation which you are so good as to express towards me, on behalf of the Danbury Baptist association, give me the highest satisfaction. My duties dictate a faithful and zealous pursuit of the interests of my constituents, & in proportion as they are persuaded of my fidelity to those duties, the discharge of them becomes more and more pleasing.
>
> Believing with you that religion is a matter which lies solely between Man & his God, that he owes account to none other for his faith or his worship, that the legitimate powers of government reach actions only, & not opinions, I contemplate with sovereign reverence that act of the whole American people which declared that their legislature should 'make

no law respecting an establishment of religion, or prohibiting the free exercise thereof,' thus building a wall of separation between Church & State. Adhering to this expression of the supreme will of the nation in behalf of the rights of conscience, I shall see with sincere satisfaction the progress of those sentiments which tend to restore to man all his natural rights, convinced he has no natural right in opposition to his social duties.

I reciprocate your kind prayers for the protection & blessing of the common father and creator of man, and tender you for yourselves & your religious association, assurances of my high respect & esteem.

Th Jefferson Jan. 1. 1802."[131]

Jefferson is consistent with all other writings contemporaneous to the Founding Documents in describing the legitimate powers of the government and, citing the text of the First Amendment, in clarifying its sole purpose is to "restore to man all his natural rights" and that that these natural rights should work in harmony with his "social duties."

Read plainly, in context, and without prior agenda, Jefferson's phrase "a wall of separation between church and state" was essentially describing the different spheres of government (civil, church, and family) that are entirely consistent with Divine Law.

Yet the *Everson* Court and the case law outflowing from 1947 took this phrase entirely out of context and built a legal doctrine that is completely inconsistent with the legitimate role of government, the text of the U.S. Constitution, and even Jefferson's own statement when read in context.

The *Everson* Court held that the Establishment Clause in the First Amendment was binding on the states also, through the Due Process Clause in the Fourteenth Amendment. The Court had taken the Fourteenth Amendment out of its legitimate context and instituted a new era of extreme federalism by taking away the states' rights and ability to establish their own laws in accordance with the U.S. Constitution (and therefore Divine Law), through clear authority secured by the Tenth Amendment.

The next step in the Sexual Revolution, after divorcing civil law from Divine Law and the utter breakdown of social values and common sense, was to allow women the "freedom of sexual expression" through any birth control methods—the issue in *Griswold*. Because the Court had to juggle a seeming adherence to the U.S. Constitution while simultaneously granting a "right" found nowhere in Divine Law or the regulatory power of federalism in the U.S. Constitution, the Penumbra Doctrine was born.

Everson and *Griswold* began the two parallel threads in the Court's "constitutional" law that worked in harmony to advance the secular humanist agenda by simultaneously attacking Religious Freedom and promoting the Sexual Revolution.

Important to our discussion of *Griswold* and the new Penumbra Doctrine, Justice Douglas (the *Griswold* majority writer) was already a member of the Court when *Everson* was decided. He remained a member of the Court until 1975 and was succeeded by Justice John Paul Stevens, himself a member of the Court until 2010.

Griswold v. Connecticut, 1965

The majority opinion stated that the specific, textual guarantees in the Bill of Rights have these "penumbras" that are "formed by emanations from those guarantees that help give them life and substance."[132]

In other words, the Court creatively redefined the directly stated role of government in the Declaration of Independence and the explicit limitation in the U.S. Constitution on the authority of the federal government, which was specifically included at the very end of the original Bill of Rights in the Tenth Amendment: "The powers not delegated to the United States by the U.S. Constitution, nor prohibited by it to the states, are reserved to the states respectively, or to the people."[133]

This Penumbra Doctrine has, since *Griswold,* been extended into the whole text of the U.S. Constitution, and has essentially given unfettered power to the Sovereign Supreme Court to read into the U.S. Constitution anything it desires. No need for actual interpretation of the U.S. Constitution or the idea that the Court is subject to its literal meaning.

The Court, by its own power of judicial review, bestowed upon itself the immeasurable ability to be the final word. When the U.S. Constitution is in conflict with their morality or any new trend in society, the justices may simply refer to the penumbra, as if they are magical legal wizards who see things that only the power of the Sovereign's crystal ball illuminates.

Law schools teach law students about this penumbra as if it is fact, completely obfuscating the *real* fact: that the Supreme Court simply fabricated the existence of a penumbra to usurp greater authority than its legitimate role in government actually conferred. Now, we can read into the U.S. Constitution any moral conclusion that the Supreme Court wants, label it a "right," and make it appear to be valid law.

This opened the floodgates to the absolute power of the Supreme Court as Sovereign, and decisions after *Griswold* were doomed to fall subject to the convergence of opinions—the personal morality and simple majority of the Nine.

Very tellingly, this doctrine and the abusive citation to the Fourteenth Amendment have been used in every landmark Supreme Court cases that have advanced the Sexual Revolution. There is no legitimate authority for these decisions on so-called "women's rights" (the propaganda label for a secular humanist narrative) and therefore the Court is forced to literally fabricate Constitutional authority.

Ironically, the very same argument that secular philosophers assert against a biblical interpretation of the original intent of the U.S. Constitution—that we cannot rest our case in the personal faith of the Founders—is the exact same argument as applied to the personal beliefs of the nine sitting justices that they applaud. We are resting our case for interpretation of the U.S. Constitution's "penumbra" in the personal values and morality of the simple majority of the current nine that happen to be sitting when an issue is decided.

This is incredible.

This dynamic is also one of the primary reasons the appointment of new Supreme Court justices is a hotly debated campaign issue during presidential election years. It is not enough that a qualified, distinguished attorney be appointed to serve. If the U.S. Constitution had a fixed, objective meaning that the Founder lawyers meant for any lawyer to understand, the composition of the Supreme Court would not be nearly so critical.

Yet the personal beliefs and track record of moral decisions of each candidate to the Supreme Court are reviewed thoroughly by Congress and the media because we all know (even if we did not understand the legal reasons) why the *personal* beliefs and the *moral* values of candidates for judicial appointments matter.[134] This is not simply about competent civil governance. It is now about the personal morality and subjective beliefs of a simple majority of the nine justices that have become our national Sovereign.

The track record of the majority opinions of the Sovereign have continued placating Social Contract Theory and espousing ideas within the shadows between the lines of the U.S. Constitution that *never* existed within the Founders' framing or the government's legitimate authority.

Lemon v. Kurtzman, 1971

Citing to a penumbra right and again taking the Fourteenth Amendment entirely out of context, the Court held that there existed a "right to privacy" under the Due Process Clause of the Fourteenth Amendment, and this privacy right extended to a woman's choice whether or not to have an abortion.

Originally in *Roe v. Wade*, the Court "balanced" this so-called right to privacy with additional terms of art—generated simply to make Constitutional Law more confusing and hide the real agenda—the "legitimate state interest" in regulating abortion laws. Thus, the Court allowed the states to give women this "right" to choose abortion, and further advancing the agenda of secular humanism, the Sexual Revolution, and feminism.

What is known as "the *Lemon* test" came from this decision and remains the standard that the Supreme Court devised to create a huge gap between objective morality and government, under the guise of "separation of church and state."[135]

Rather than the plain meaning of the First Amendment's Establishment Clause simply guaranteeing that Congress could not set up a national religion (comparative to the Church of England where the King of England is the head of the church), and individuals were free to practice their faith, the Court went a huge step further and decided that the role of civil government could not overlap whatsoever with the church's government.

Lemon constructed a three-part test for government action:

1. Government action must have a secular purpose
2. Government action must not have the primary effect of advancing or inhibiting religion
3. Government action must not have "excessive entanglement" with religion

Consider how *vastly* different this "test" is to the proper role of government as defined by the Founders!

This case set the foundation for the Supreme Court to impose what Pearcey defines as the "secular / sacred split"[136]—the idea (again, moral judgment) that science is amoral and that only amoral science may be taught in public schools.

However, as we continue to see, this so-called "secular" purpose that *Lemon* demands is merely a lofty term for *subjective* morality, imposed by secular humanist theory and a Sovereign Supreme Court. The Court has not ceased to issue moral judgments or demand that any other moral viewpoint be stricken from the government sector (particularly public schools).

This is simply a legal fiction to impose the Sovereign's changing and subjective morality on the nation.

Roe v. Wade, 1973

As more women were "liberated" into a life of promiscuity and sex was openly discussed in colleges, in magazines, and even in churches, women whose birth control failed them needed abortion as a birth control alternative.

We see this subjective moral judgment very clearly in the decision of the Sovereign Supreme to value the "rights" of the mother over the unborn child's unalienable Right to life.[137] Appealing to the fluid nature of subjective morality rather than the right to *life* endowed by God and textually acknowledged in the U.S. Constitution, Declaration of Independence, and Divine Law itself, the Supreme Court imposed its own moral judgment. The Court usurped its legitimate authority by believing it had the power to grant and therefore take away the unalienable right to life.

There is irrefutable empirical scientific evidence that shows life beginning at conception, but we now do not call that "life" but rather a "fetus" or "embryo" as though changing the terms makes something less a scientific and moral fact than it is. Through Judicial Activism, the Supreme Court creatively redefined "life" and ignored fixed, objective, universal moral principles in favor of the changing views of a partial segment of society.

The natural consequences of the Sexual Revolution are an increase in pregnancies. Feminists taught that women should be able to "have sex like men" and in order to remove all natural consequences of this illicit behavior, women had to be legally able to terminate unwanted pregnancies through abortion.

One feminist author blatantly pushed the secular humanist agenda in a New York Times Op-Ed and wrote,

> "We need to say that women have sex, have abortions, are at peace with the decision and move on with their lives. We need to say that is their right, and, moreover, it's good for everyone that they have this right: The whole society benefits when motherhood is voluntary. When we gloss over these truths we unintentionally promote the stigma we're trying to combat. What, you didn't agonize? You forgot your pill? You just didn't want to have a baby now? You should be ashamed of yourself."[138]

The Women's Rights Movement, through Planned Parenthood and the National Organization of Women, demanded that women have a "right" to choose and "rights" over their bodies in ways that are completely against natural consequences of sexual behavior and against objective morality and biblical commands. Clearly, the right to choose abortion is not a Constitutional right because it is against Divine Law and also because it is against the directly stated right to life enumerated in the Declaration of Independence as unalienable.

Yet, through the rights "emanating from the penumbra" in the U.S. Constitution, the Supreme Sovereign again held a fluid, subjective standard and imposed its own morality, replacing universal morality. Interestingly, Justice Douglas from the *Griswold* Court was still a member of the Court and joined the majority opinion in *Roe*.

The majority of the Court adhered to its now usual practice by citing the "right of privacy" located somewhere in the penumbra of the Fourteenth Amendment. The majority insisted that the "right of privacy…in the Fourteenth Amendment's concept of personal liberty…is broad enough to encompass a woman's decision whether or not to terminate her pregnancy."[139]

In keeping with the rationale of *Everson* more than two decades prior, the Court read into the U.S. Constitution this fundamental right, a guarantee of "personal privacy." As a fundamental right, any state law regulating or limiting abortions had to be justified by a "compelling state interest"—as if the state interest in Divine Law morality is not compelling enough!

Unfortunately, rather than understanding, articulating, and arguing the illegitimate *basis* of this Supreme Court opinion in secular humanism, the greater evangelical community has allowed the debate to be framed within a Social Contract Theory perspective. We argue pro-choice vs. pro-life and whose personal beliefs should be imposed on the whole, largely predicated in the majority of society's whim.

One cartoon aptly showed the head–to–head problem of this approach, depicting two rams butting heads and pushing against each other from an equally-footed position. One ram was labeled "Pro-Life" and the other labeled "Pro-Choice." We will not make any headway with this kind of posture. If we simply stress that the sanctity of life is a compelling state interest and argue this issue within the Social Contract Theory definitions and terms, we have already lost all objective moral grounding and thus, the whole debate.

Roe still placed some limitations on abortions, including a "point of viability" within the third trimester of pregnancy and affirming the state's interest in this "potential life," and the states could still prohibit abortions within the third trimester to protect "potential life."

The Court even stated that the primary right advanced by its opinion was the physician's right to practice medicine (absent the state's "compelling interest") rather than the mother's right to choose or right to privacy.

One Justice later observed, "… I have concluded that the end of the first trimester is critical. This is arbitrary, but perhaps any other selected point, such as quickening or viability, is equally arbitrary."[140]

However, the *Roe* basis in subjective morality and penumbra rights continued to advance despite this concededly arbitrary definition, and in the 1992 *Planned Parenthood v. Casey* opinion, the Supreme Court explicitly decided women had a "constitutional right" to abortion. While *Casey* retained *Roe's* basic premise—abortion on demand—it completely *Roe's* "trimester" rationale in favor of an equally arbitrary and far more pro-choice satisfactory "vitality" framework. [141]

The Court again cited to and abused the Fourteenth Amendment, declaring that this "right" was rooted in the Fourteenth Amendment's due process clause and "emanating from the vast penumbra."

As the Sexual Revolution advanced and became even more socially acceptable, the Supreme Court Sovereign had to keep up and declare the bare will of the majority without regard to its limitation of being *under* the U.S. Constitution and Divine Law's authority.

Author and attorney Mark Levin makes the valid point that we are now living in a "post-Constitutional country."[142] This is entirely true.

It is worth mentioning here that Americans have also largely been confused on the appropriate definition of our government as a construct. We are not a democracy—we are a constitutional republic.

In fact, the U.S. Constitution specifically states this fact in Article IV in what is known as the Guarantee Clause.[143] This clause states that the federal government shall guarantee to the states a republican form of government. That is, that the "consent of the governed" will be effectuated through a trustee form of government and *representatives* of government—not direct democracy and simple majority.

The proper operation of this clause is very similar to how the Electoral College functions. The simple popular majority of the people's will is an illegitimate authority for governance. In fact, the Greek word for democracy is "dimokratia" or "force of the people" and meaning a "mob rule." This is specifically the type of rule the Founders intended to avoid through a representative form of government. The Founders even avoided direct democracy for the procedure electing our officers of government in the federal Executive and Judiciary branches.

City of Boerne v. Flores, 1997

Possibly the least well-known Constitutional Law case among those discussed here to non-attorneys, *City of Boerne v. Flores*[144] was one of the most significant usurpations of Supreme Court authority and another evolution into the growing power of a Supreme Sovereign.

The context of this case centered upon the Religious Freedom Restoration Act (RFRA), crafted and enacted by Congress as a direct response to the Supreme Court's opinion in *Employment Division v. Smith*[145] (wherein, against a First Amendment challenge, and Oregon law criminalizing peyote use in Native American religious rituals was upheld). States became concerned that this opinion would be cited as precedent to encroach upon other forms of religious freedom expression and eventually regulate religious practices, and in response to the states' lobby, Congress enacted the RFRA.

The Supreme Court ultimately struck down the RFRA as unconstitutional in *Flores*. But the most important outcome of this case in terms of precedent was the idea presumptively asserted in dicta that the Court holds the sole power to define the substantive rights guaranteed by the Fourteenth Amendment, and Congress's enforcement power cannot be used to contradict a Supreme Court interpretation of the Fourteenth Amendment.

Thus, while the actual text of the Due Process Clause prohibits deprivation of life, liberty, or property without legislative authorization, the Court chose to magnify judicial review so that Congress and the states do not hold the textual power to legislatively authorize any opinion against the Supreme Court.

The Supreme Court gained even more power by virtue of its own declaration, without any additional oversight or accountability.

This was a clear act of Judicial Activism and a usurpation of government authority granted to the other branches of government through the U.S. Constitution by the separation of powers.

So while the practical application was a general and broad limit on Congressional powers and a bold move to make the Legislative Branch entirely subservient to the Court's own powers, the Court fashioned this decision while determining whether Congress had power to legislate for religious freedoms, showing again its secular humanist agenda.

Lawrence v. Texas, 2003

Continuing the expanse and open advocacy of the moral conclusions asserted by the Sexual Revolution and under the guise of a "right to privacy" that "emanates from the vast penumbra," the Supreme Court Sovereign declared same-sex sexual activity legal.[146]

The Court overturned its own previous holding on this same issue (and same contemplated "privacy right" within sexual activity) in the 1986 case *Bowers v. Hardwick*.[147] That case had specifically stated that the Court found no constitutional rights or protections within sexual activity privacy.

But, the advancing foothold of the Sexual Revolution was demanding that every person be free to express his or her sexuality in *any* form. The war on women's rights had won birth control and abortion; now the battleground was for open homosexuality, transgender, and polyamorous activity.

The majority opinion, written by Justice Kennedy (the same Justice Kennedy that wrote the majority opinion in *Obergefell*), stated, "The petitioners are entitled to respect for their private lives. The State cannot demean their existence or control their destiny by making their private sexual conduct a crime."

He went on to state that *Bowers* was not correct and "now is overruled," also holding that the rationale for the majority in *Lawrence* was through the Fourteenth Amendment.

"The Texas statute [against sodomy—at issue in *Lawrence*] furthers no legitimate state interest which can justify its intrusion into the personal and private life of the individual," wrote Kennedy, weaving through the parallel strands set up decades earlier by *Griswold* and *Lemon*.

As sex education classes began as early as kindergarten in schools, questioning one's heterosexuality became the norm and celebrated as the next mutation of "liberation." Schools now even encourage kindergarten-aged school children to dress in opposite gender's clothing to "liberate" them from gender bias and attempt to discover what gender the child relates to more.

This case set the groundwork for open celebration of homosexuality and all kinds of deviant sexual behavior with any coupling or grouping. The next decade would see the rise of gender neutrality and redefinition of "personhood"—the next phase of the Sexual Revolution and the attempt to remove any inherent sexuality and gender from a person at birth.

Van Orden v. Perry, 2005

The parallel strand of war on Religious Freedom has kept pushing along, and this case was a significant loss. *Van Orden v. Perry* is particularly worth mentioning because the evangelical community often misinterprets this as a 'win' against separation of church and state. This is because the ultimate conclusion of the case was to allow the Ten Commandments to be displayed on the grounds of the Texas State Capitol.[148]

That seems like a win.

However, the reasoning of the Court's opinion was anything but supportive of objective morality and tearing down the fictitious "wall of separation." Justice Brever reasoned in a concurring opinion that the Ten Commandments display must be considered in context and served an "historical" and "secular" purpose:

"...the Commandments' text on this monument conveys a predominately secular message [...] and historical message reflective of a cultural heritage."[149]

Van Orden was decided the same day that a nearly identical issue was decided by the Court in a companion case, *McCreary County v. ACLU of Kentucky*.[150] The Court decided *McCreary* seemingly completely opposite to *Van Orden*. But again, the rationale is the key. The same issue was before the Court—the secular or sacred purpose of a religious display and its Constitutionality under the First Amendment (or, as the First Amendment had now been perverted to be under the *Lemon* test).

In these cases, the Court dealt with two Ten Commandments displays at two courthouses in Kentucky, and the outcome turned on the historical context of how the displays came to be positioned at their respective locations and ultimately the purpose that they served—secular or sacred. Thus, unlike in *Van Orden*, the Court applied the *Lemon* test and concluded that the displays in *McCreary* were unconstitutional. The Court stated that in applying the *Lemon* test any government action "with the ostensible and predominant purpose of advancing religion"[151] violates the Establishment Clause in the First Amendment.

But the point is that both of these cases apply the fundamentally unconstitutional *Lemon* test and both equally assert that church and state are separate and that government may only act with a secular purpose. While *Lemon* has fallen out of favor as the primary test, a secular vs. sacred divide and purpose continues to be the Supreme Court standard for First Amendment religious cases. We must be very careful how we read Court opinions and look at the basis and reasoning for the decision—not simply review the ultimate outcome of the issue.

Obergefell v. Hodges, 2015

Next, marriage itself and the traditional morality that sets the foundation for family and the sphere of government essential to a moral and upright society were redefined.[152]

Attorney and law professor Michael Schutt commented, "[T]he most troubling aspect of *Obergefell* is what it says about the law itself and what that means for the future of the rule of law in America. This decision was *not* based on law—in fact, it had nothing to do with the law. The case was decided, instead, on pure will: the political and social preferences of five justices on the Supreme Court."[153]

It is a chilling observation that each of these decisions and nearly all of the important, primary departures from objective morality and fashioning new "rights" within the penumbra deals with issues specifically related to the Sexual Revolution: divorcing morality from education, contraception, abortion, sexual privacy, same-sex marriage, and the list goes on. Society wanted sexual freedom and the only way to achieve that was through legal declarations masquerading as "rights."

We have been completely misled into believing the bases of these Supreme Court decisions are to effectuate these so-called fundamental rights and are pro-women, but these "rights" are humanist, immoral, and nothing more than blatant embrace of the Sexual Revolution.

Women are actually being exploited worse today than prior to the 1940's—women are encouraged in the name of "empowerment" to "have sex like men" (no commitment, no partnership), tear apart their bodies with abortions, face the often unhealthy consequences (including infertility) of contraception, and more—all in the name of "liberation" and "equality."

Other laws have evolved based on Social Contract Theory that has pervaded objective morality, including Domestic Relations laws.

Many states have no-fault divorces, adultery is now legal (and even celebrated through polyamory), and women continue to be fed the lies that motherhood is somehow less than desirable and pregnancy is merely a biological function that can be easily alleviated.

The Sexual Revolution continues to pervade normative social mores and we are seeing more and more headlines about gender and transgender selection, blurred lines between a "fetus" and "personhood" and between male and female, polyamory, homosexuality, and fewer Millennial men and women choosing to marry or have children and certainly even fewer doing so within the context of a traditional nuclear family.

Within the next decade or sooner, polygamy and polyamory will be the next target goal and the "right" to sexual privacy and the "right" to licensing will extend not just to couplings but also to groupings. Sexual expression will continue to pervade any sense of boundaries or morality, and the homosexual slogan "love is love" will become the mantra of the pedophile. Gender and personhood will continue to be attacked and redefined as transgender lifestyles and "gender identification" are lauded in mainstream media as courageous.

All of this is a consequence of the full embrace and celebration of the Sexual Revolution, the Social Contract Theory, and secular humanism. Over the past 60-plus years, the Supreme Court has sought to cut off the U.S. Constitution from its legitimate Founding Documents Hierarchy and instead place it onto a Social Contract Theory foundation, completely antithetical to its original foundation in Divine Law.

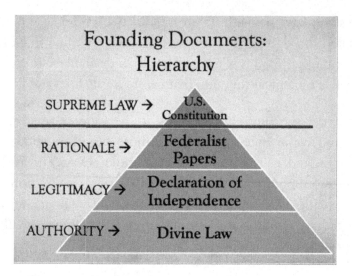

Cutting off U.S Constitution and replacing it onto Social Contract

The Supreme Court Sovereign, even including the more conservative justices, has completely bought into the lie of the Sexual Revolution, the separation of church and state, and the legal fiction that is an outgrowth of the secular humanist worldview.

CHAPTER 11

ON DISCOVERABLE MORALITY

"I've lived, Sir, a long time, and the longer I live, the more convincing
Proofs I see of this Truth—That God governs in the affairs of men.
And if a sparrow cannot fall to the ground without His notice,
is it probable that an Empire can rise without His aid?"[154]

- Benjamin Franklin

It is prudent to include a brief commentary showing how morality is fixed, discoverable law. This is central to where we go from here and *how* to interpret the U.S. Constitution consistent with Divine Law. Morality is not just a nice philosophical theory to support a religious argument or to advocate for religious freedom.

Divine Law, supported by biblical truth, encompasses the *whole* Truth of reality—general revelation. As Schaeffer said, "Christianity is not a series of truths in the plural, but rather truth spelled with a capital "T." Truth about total reality, not just about religious things. Biblical Christianity is Truth concerning total reality—and the intellectual holding of that total Truth and then living in the light of that Truth."[155]

If we are to take seriously the proper foundations of legitimate jurisprudence in Divine Law, we must be able to apply this Truth in a practical form.

Each of us intuitively and mysteriously understands basic universal laws of morality and knows them as perceptively as we do laws of science that control us physically. For example, even if we can't describe them intellectually, we still perceived gravity before we knew its intellectual label. Yet, atheist philosophers, including secular humanists, still assert the notion that morality is purely social and exists only within the realm of the *statutory construct*. Importantly, this argument concedes that morality *is* perceivable. Just not objectively determinable.

This is a critical distinction in debating objective morality.

The cultural narrative has divorced facts and science from morality, consistently pushing the idea that we each have our own morality (and reality). Yet we see this is inconsistent even with man's own nature (the supposed root of all reality for the secular humanist) and our perceptive awareness and knowledge of moral law's existence. C.S. Lewis described this as the "Law of Human Nature" and provided an excellent example:

> "Everyone has heard people quarrelling. Sometimes it sounds funny and sometimes it sounds merely unpleasant; but however it sounds, I believe we can learn something very important from listening to the kind of things they say. They say things like this: 'How'd you like it if anyone did the same to you?'— 'That's my seat, I was here first'—'Leave him alone, he isn't doing you any harm'—'Why should you shove in first?'—'Give me a bit of your orange, I gave you a bit of mine'—'Come on, you promised.' People say things like that every day, educated people as well as

uneducated, and children as well as grown-ups. Now
what interests me about all these remarks is that the
man who makes them is not merely saying that the
other man's behavior does not happen to please him.
He is appealing to some kind of standard of behavior
which he expects the other man to know about. And
the other man very seldom replies: 'To hell with your
standard.' Nearly always he tries to make out that
what he has been doing does not really go against
the standard, or that if it does there is some special
excuse. … It looks, in fact, very much as if both
parties had in mind some kind of Law or Rule of fair
play or decent behavior or morality, or whatever you
like to call it, about which they really agreed. And
they have. If they had not…they could not quarrel
in the human sense of the word. Quarrelling means
trying to show that the other man is in the wrong.
And there would be no sense in trying to do that
unless you and he had some sort of agreement as to
what Right and Wrong are[.]"[156]

As Lewis observed, this universal morality was originally labeled and
understood to be the "law of nature" because it was self-evident. We
all have a basic, perceptible understanding of morality, not because
of social conditioning or political geography, but rather because
morality exists in the world. How then have we come to separate
morality from science?

During the July 2015 historical New Horizons flyby of Pluto, the
missions operations manager Alice Bowman said something in
response to a discussion of New Horizons' extended mission that
gives us a clue about our *current* understanding of what "science"
means: "It [the satellite] was happy to go on to collect more science."
This statement is quite telling how NASA defines the term "science"
and, more importantly, how our cultural common understanding

of this term has evolved, as secular humanism has taken more firm grounding in America's cultural pulse.

Pearcey points out that during the time of the American Revolution, the term "science" was not confined to physical matter:

> "It is important to realize that the term *science* had not yet acquired the narrow, specialized meaning it has today. Instead, it meant any form of systematized knowledge (Latin for *knowledge* is *scientia*), so that term was applied even to subjects like politics, morality, and theology ("the queen of the sciences"). This explains why so many clergymen at the time assumed that a scientific method like [Sir Francis] Bacon's could be applied to theology. It did not necessarily mean they were selling out to scientism, as some critics have suggested. It did mean, however, that they were seeking to meet the challenge of modern science in part by arguing that theology followed the same inductive method."[157]

Universal morality is just as determinable as other forms of science, when properly understood to be knowledge. Knowledge is information regarding truth. We can and already do have information on the truth and existence of universal morality.

Discoverable knowledge is sometimes *but not always* empirical. "Empirical" really just means measurable by one of the five senses. But there are ways to measure and obtain knowledge through some objective system other than the human senses, and science itself recognizes this. We have a lot of knowledge that is not empirically observed.

For example, think about the concepts of numbers or time. We know these phenomena exist because we can see their effects and they are logically derived from their effects on the physical world. But we cannot empirically observe "number" as a concept, or even "time." We can measure and observe the effects of time on physical reality and we can logically understand the concept of numbers and label the "effect" of numerical grouping or ordering. No one would dispute the existence of numbers simply because we cannot see, touch, feel, or otherwise sense the concept of them, inferred from our physical universe.

The same is absolutely true for the concept and logical existence of morality.

Additionally, much of science is not observable to man himself through his own senses, and must be understood with assistance of technology (like New Horizons—we saw Pluto close up through the assistance of the satellite—we did not empirically observe it organically through only our senses). Some scientific truth is not actually ever physically observable through the senses.

An example of this is the concept of other dimensions beyond those empirically perceptible to humans in our physical universe. We know that there are more dimensions than we are able to empirically perceive, largely because multidimensional mathematics has been developed to represent a framework for this knowledge, and though we do not know precisely what number of dimensions there are, this framework of scientific truth has helped scientists describe the physical world.

Similarly, morality does not have to be empirically observed to exist, particularly when we do perceive and observe its effects and have a logical framework to understand why it exists. The term "morality" itself is a framework and description to enable us to label and describe the truth that we observe to exist in the world.

Morality, principally, is the distinction between what is right and wrong, good and evil.

Morality then as a scientific term is established on the existence of right and wrong, good and evil. We know and perceive the existence of good and evil in the universe. One, by definition, cannot exist without the other. The reason we know something is good is because of the contrast to those other things that are evil.

Morality can also be discovered through measurable means, through its effect on physical reality, and through the fact that it is also science. We often debate the existence of the moral spectrum from the standpoint of arguing whether a specific act is good or bad. Importantly, whatever the truth about that specific act's goodness, that conclusion does not prove or disprove the existence of the spectrum.

When we are debating a moral issue, we have already inherently agreed that there does exist morality: good and evil, right and wrong. We might argue where to place a certain shade of red on the visible light spectrum, but we are fundamentally agreeing that there is a spectrum of visible light to begin with.

The idea that we can argue over where to place certain acts within the moral spectrum simply suggests that we do not as readily perceive the consequences of the truth of the moral act's placement on the spectrum as readily and immediately as we do other scientific laws.

As C.S. Lewis observed, man can choose to disobey moral law in ways he cannot choose to disobey physical laws:

> "We may put this in another way. Each man is at every moment subjected to several different sets of law but there is only one of these which he is free to disobey. As a body, he is subjected to gravitation and cannot disobey it; if you leave him unsupported in mid-air, he has no more choice about falling than a stone has. As an organism, he is subjected to various biological laws which he cannot disobey any more

than an animal can. That is, he cannot disobey those laws which he shares with other things; but the law which is peculiar to his human nature, the law he does not share with animals or vegetables or inorganic things, is the one he can disobey if he chooses."[158]

But this very important point is present in Lewis's observation—morality is still there as a fixed, discoverable law, even though the laws of the universe are fixed in such a way we can choose to disobey it.

Further, just because we cannot observe the mechanism by which a physical law works does not mean that the science itself does not exist. Humans saw color existing long before they understood the spectrum of light and understood the mechanism of measuring light waves. This intrinsic aspect of color being founded completely in the light spectrum existed and occurred before humans knew it existed or understood it or discovered its relationship to perceivable color.

We did not invent it, we did not legislate it, we merely began to understand how to measure it and why color, as we perceive it, existed. Color also exists regardless of the blind man's inability to perceive it with his other working senses.

Determinable consequences of choosing to go against moral law are still inherently present and fixed within the reality of objective morality. Simply because we do not immediately perceive the consequence does not mean that it's not going to happen or if a "bad" consequences does not measurably happen, that means the act was right. In the reality of the construct of our world, moral law is not enforced similarly to physical law—there is not an immediate cause and effect.

But similarly to statutory law, someone could get away with committing the crime of rape (against moral law also) and successfully hide from civil justice for years before the consequences eventually occur. Lack of civil justice does not equal civil rightness. In the same way, lack of moral justice does not equal moral rightness.

We do see some immediate cause and effect and some long-term cause and effect of moral rightness and moral wrongness. These perceptions, additionally to what we know about basic moral principles, help guide us to more and more clearly understand the spectrum of universal morality.

As U.S. Constitutional attorney Bryan Beauman wrote,

> "In reality, it is difficult to identify *any* law that contains no moral component. Laws preventing animal cruelty or environmental destruction, for instance, derive from a sense of humanity's moral interaction with other living things and natural resources. And does anyone seriously believe that laws preventing human sex trafficking are flawed because they are based on a moral ethos? Laws are motivated by a number of moral concerns, including the protection of life, liberty, and property. Frequently, advocates on *both* sides of a legal issue, such as capital punishment, support their positions with moral arguments. So the question is really not *whether* we should legislate morality, but *whose* morality we will legislate."[159]

In this universal, discoverable sense, we advocate for biblical principles and biblical concepts of morality. This is not *just* because we believe in the Bible's truth according to our Christianity, but because biblical principles are consistent with Divine Law's general revelation and the Bible itself is a specific revelation from God so that we might know more about the metaphysical reality (including morality) than we might discover on our own through general revelation.

The Bible is our moral New Horizons—the functional assistance by which we view and more clearly see objective morality, its spectrum, and further explain and gain knowledge about our universe. We do not need the Bible to perceive objective morality and general revelation, but with the assistance of this incredible lens, much more objective Truth comes into focus than we could ever observe by ourselves.

The Bible itself speaks to this: "They know the truth about God because He has made it obvious to them. For since the world was created, people have seen the earth and sky. Through everything God made, they can clearly see His invisible qualities—His eternal power and divine nature. So they have no excuse for not knowing God."[160]

In other words, God has given us the ability to discover His "invisible" qualities (including morality), by and through general revelation, which includes these qualities as well as what man *can* empirically observe—for example, the earth and sky. "The heavens declare the glory of God, and the firmament shows His handiwork."[161]

Morality, the concept of discerning between right and wrong, is absolutely universal and discoverable.

CHAPTER 12

RELIGIOUS FREEDOM AND THE U.S. CONSTITUTION

"The Christian religion is the basis, or rather the source, of all genuine freedom in government... I am persuaded that no civil government of a republican form can exist and be durable in which the principles of Christianity have not a controlling influence."[162]

"No truth is more evident to my mind than that the Christian religion must be the basis of any government intended to secure the rights and privileges of a free people...and in this indispensible obligation of all men to yield entire obedience to God's commands in the moral law and the Gospel."[163]

- Judge Noah Webster

Most Americans understand that the First Amendment to the U.S. Constitution guarantees at least some form of the generally understood concepts of Freedom of Religion and Free Exercise of Religion and that these guarantees are being systematically attacked.

For a comprehensive analysis, it's important to unpack the thread of Religious Freedom independently from the Sexual Revolution discussion. Religious Freedom has been attacked directly by Judicial

Activists and secular humanists, both in active government and latent academia.

One of the most understandably feared results stemming from *Obergefell* is what that decision will ultimately mean for churches, faith-based organizations, and individual Christians. These fears were given life in the various dissenting opinions.

As one commentator observed, "Four themes have emerged from these [dissenting] justices:

- The U.S. Constitution is silent on the issue of same-sex marriage
- The People, not the courts, should decide the issue of marriage through democratic means
- This decision poses a threat to religious freedom
- The opinions of five justices should not decide matters of policy for the entire country"[164]

The dissent got three of the four issues correct—Divine Law, not the states through democratic majority, should decide the issue of marriage. As we have just discussed, we are a constitutional republic, built on the solid foundation of Divine Law principles.

Initially, we must go back to the actual meaning of religious freedom within the First Amendment. As the beginning of the Bill of Rights, the First Amendment states:

> *Congress shall make no law respecting an establishment of religion, or prohibiting the free exercise thereof; or abridging the freedom of speech, or of the press; or the right of the people to peaceably assemble, and to petition the Government for a redress of grievances.*[165]

The text of this initial series of rights specifically outlined by the Founder lawyers presents several observations:

First, Congress was the only branch contemplated to be making the law—*not* the Judicial Branch. When the Founder lawyers included the Bill of Rights (over Hamilton's objection), the Judicial Branch did not yet have the authority of judicial review. The Founders presumed and intended that the only lawmaker would be the Legislative Branch.

Second, government (via Congress) is the only actor that the Amendment restrains. The First Amendment accomplishes the two-fold purpose of restraining *government* action while acknowledging the individual inalienable right to free exercise of religion, freedom of speech, freedom of the press, freedom of association, and freedom of petitioning the government.

There were purposefully no limitations on these freedoms because any legitimate limitation through government would *already* necessarily have to conform with Divine Law—for example, a law that prohibited exercising one's religion through child sacrifice.

A common misunderstanding of Religious Freedom is that it is unlimited. It *is* limited. But the First Amendment is not talking about what we as individuals CAN do, but rather what the government CANNOT do. This is not a "separation of church and state" but rather an acknowledgement of the overlapping spheres of government and also the proper role of government: securing unalienable rights that exist independent of government fiat or assistance.

The government is not the grantor, provider, or source of Religious Freedom, and therefore does *not* have the authority to restrict it *other than* appropriate contextual laws that conform to Divine Law.

For example, consider the other amendments in the Bill of Rights that discuss a criminal defendant's fundamental rights (found in the Fourth, Fifth, Sixth, and Eighth Amendments). In context, these rights are absolutely unalienable, but even effectively applied, a criminal defendant may still be found guilty within the government's proper criminal justice role.

If we go back to Federalist No. 84 and remember Hamilton's discussion of why a Bill of Rights is unnecessary, we should consider how our notion of Religious Freedom would (and would not) change if the Bill of Rights was not included in the U.S. Constitution. Since, as Hamilton argued, the Bill of Rights was unnecessary, an understanding of what rights are unalienable (and what are actual rights) must be derived from something other than a collective majority of commentators—a legitimate authority.

We know by this point that the legitimate authority is exclusively Divine Law. So the First Amendment and the entirety of the Bill of Rights must be in conformance with Divine Law—*and* any interpretation of Constitutional law.

Rights are those things which the Declaration of Independence has already stipulated and assented are "unalienable" and given by the Creator. Obviously, the Creator would not endow rights that contravene His own doctrine and Divine Law principles. "Rights" therefore are not that difficult to discover and understand, and are certainly not found within the shadowy penumbra that a legal scholar has fabricated solely by virtue of his or her place on the Sovereign bench.

The U.S. Constitution is silent on some things. It could not sensibly be comprehensive to a degree that textually includes commentary literally on every subject or on issues brought about by advancement in technology. However, that does not mean that these issues are "hidden" within the vast penumbra of the U.S. Constitution. That is just as absurd as saying that the Founders textually discussed regulations on cell phone privacy. That technology simply did not exist for the Founders to specifically discuss if they believed it necessary.

So what *does* this mean?

We must see what the text of the U.S. Constitution says in context and connection with what the other Founding Documents say and what principles are logically derived from these sources that provide guidance for later unresolved issues.

Divine Law and objective morality are the standards by which we must determine the legitimate authority of the government and the correct interpretation of the U.S. Constitution, including Religious Freedom. The so-called "right" to marry is *only* within the context of Divine Law. The so-called "women's rights" are *only* within the sphere of Divine Law. The actual right to life of conceived and unborn children stems from Divine Law.

Religious Freedom is not a limited tolerance for faith-based communities and an absolute tolerance for any expression of so-called "religion"—including redefining marriage, overhaul of sexual morality, etc. Religious Freedom is a direct outflow of Divine Law, the church as a coequal sphere of government, and acknowledgement of our Creator who endowed these inalienable rights.

"Religious Freedom" is another term of art that has been creatively reinterpreted by the secular humanist agenda and effectuated by the Supreme Sovereign to mean that the government has authority to compartmentalize and sanitize religion from any government-funded agency.

An interesting by-product (or collateral consequence) of the rise of social media and privatized press and the blogosphere is that big corporations can effectively abridge religious freedom (via regulating the freedom of speech or the press) through their own rules. Consider Facebook, the ultimate social media page, where anyone's written speech is published to his or her audience. Because Facebook is *not* a government agent, it can and does restrict and remove content at its own sheer discretion.

A huge misnomer of this type of restriction on free speech and publication is that users can assert First Amendment rights against corporations. This is false. *Corporate* action is not covered by Constitutional authority and does not reach First Amendment breach—the U.S. Constitution contemplates only *government* action.

The impact of these large-scale corporate restrictions is that the largest forums for public speech are controlled. Unlike the "legalese" posted and reposted on personal pages claiming to own content on one's personal page, the contractual agreement that is signed by each user when opening their account dictates that Facebook owns the content and basically can in its sole discretion restrict whatever content it deems violates its rules.

This is a problem when corporations that advance the secular humanist narrative and agenda control these information and public forums. On June 26, 2015—the day the *Obergefell* decision was handed down—Facebook offered a free service for users to create a rainbow flag overlay to their profile pictures. It offered no such reciprocal service to users wishing to publicly declare their opposition. But under current law, it does not have to.

One of the latent and most immediate threats to Religious Freedom is in this form of corporate abridging of the press—an issue that the First Amendment is intentionally silent on because the U.S. Constitution's function is only to give limited regulatory powers to government. With the rise of corporate regulation, faith-based organizations must ensure that their voice is heard and effectively published.

Society, through embracing of the secular humanist agenda, has turned the terms of art "judgment" and "discrimination" on their head and reinvented them to be wholly negative in a cultural sense rather than retaining their original legal meaning.

"Judgment" in the legal sense is the appropriate application of rules to facts and rendering a final order on a matter. Now, the secular humanist narrative tells us that we cannot tolerate Religious Freedom because we must tolerate absolutely everyone. If Christians take Divine Law principles and apply them appropriately to facts, we are being "judgmental," which is not allowed. Yet, though an individual may not have enforcement capacity, judgment and discernment is exactly what we *should* do. That is exactly what lawyers ask juries to do every day in the courtroom—apply rules to facts and render a judgment.

But in the new mantra of tolerance and the Social Contract Theory, every man is his own individual and lives in his own reality. Judgment is intolerable, as is discrimination.

Oddly, we discriminate every day in ways that are perfectly acceptable—we choose what restaurant we will dine at, what person we will date or marry, what friends we will associate with, and the list goes on. All of these actions involve some form of discrimination, or *choosing* one option above another. It used be a compliment in the days of old to say that someone "had discriminating taste."

Yet discrimination is now a bad word. "Discrimination" in nearly any form is not tolerated, even if justified. Why? It has become another term of art largely misunderstood—and reinvented as squarely antithetical to the secular humanist notion of "equality."

The secular humanist agenda has taken these key terms of art that have a *moral* premise (good vs. bad) and have turned them all into negatives and intolerable exercises in morality.

Is it not plain to see how the objective moral basis for constitutional interpretation has been completely eroded and substituted for subjective amorality? Religious Freedom is not an arcane, dwindling concession from government that can be regulated and altogether removed at the government's will. Religious Freedom is fully grounded in the

Founding Documents Hierarchy and is an unalienable right endowed by God through Divine Law and enshrined in the U.S. Constitution merely as an acknowledgment of its existence.

Yet American Constitutional Law is going the way of the Canadian court that opined, "These shared values – equality, human rights and democracy – are values the state always has a legitimate interest in promoting and protecting. [...] Religious freedom must therefore be understood in the context of a secular, multicultural and democratic society with a strong interest in protecting dignity and diversity, promoting equality, and ensuring the vitality of a common belief in human rights."[166]

Vital to our protection and advocacy for continued Religious Freedom in the way the Founder lawyers intended is the understanding of where this right and freedom is derived, what these terms of art truly mean, and what role the government legitimately has in securing and not usurping these rights. Remember the Founding Documents Hierarchy:

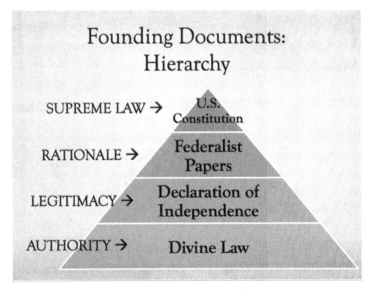

Founding Documents Hierarchy (complete)

---·**CHAPTER 13**·---

RECLAIMING THE MORAL BASIS OF U.S. CONSTITUTIONAL INTERPRETATION AND LAW

"The basis of our political systems is the right of the people
to make and to alter their constitutions of government.
But the Constitution, which at any time exists, 'till changed
by an explicit and authentic act of the whole people,
is sacredly obligatory upon all.

If in the opinion of the people the distribution or modification
of the constitutional powers be in any particular wrong, let it be
corrected by an amendment in the way which the Constitution
designates. But let there be no change by usurpation; for though
this in one instance may be the instrument of good, it is the
customary weapon by which free governments are destroyed." [167]

- George Washington

In his book *By The People*, popular political crisis author and social scientist Charles Murray states, "...that we are at the end of the American project as the founders intended it, but that opportunities are opening for preserving the best qualities of the American project in a new incarnation."[168]

The latter half of this proposition is correct. As more Americans become increasingly dissatisfied with our Sovereign and begin to pay attention and educate themselves on the truth of our roots, the question naturally becomes, *What should we do now?*

Answers range from increased apathy and hopelessness—"We're just moving to Canada, guys!"—to extremes in civil disobedience and a complete overhaul of this "American project" through a second Revolution. However, neither of those extremes are the realistic response or the most compatible and consistent with Divine Law.

Pragmatically, there is no Mayflower to sail to a New World and start a new American experiment in Divine Law self-government. Canada, from a perspective of cultural morality, is actually worse off than we are, as earlier indicated.

While each of these extremes might accomplish the end goal of throwing off the current government regime, it is vital to remember that preciously held admonishment from the Founders in the Declaration of Independence itself—civil disobedience (in the form of secession or revolt) is to be the *last* resort. There is a reason Dr. Martin Luther King Jr's writings were called "Letters from a Birmingham *Jail*" rather than a Birmingham front porch.

Yet, legal scholars, church leaders, and even state legislatures throughout America are still standing up in defiance of the latest Supreme Court opinion in *Obergefell*. In the quick aftermath of that decision, more than sixty legal scholars published a statement through the American Principles Project in defiance of the Supreme Court's overreach and patent unconstitutional overreach. This statement said in part:

> "We stand with James Madison and Abraham Lincoln
> in recognizing that the Constitution is not whatever
> a majority of Supreme Court justices say it is," the
> statement proclaimed. "We remind all officeholders
> in the United States that they are pledged to *uphold*
> the Constitution of the United States, not the will of
> five members of the Supreme Court."[169]

This statement is absolutely correct. However, we have seen throughout the last few decades and ever more increasingly each year how an overreaching federal court has become the arbiter of American morality and culture. This is quite literally the proverbial fox guarding the hen house. Isolated or even group incidents of defiance have thus far been met with swift federal action to quell the "rebellion." This is certainly an option, but likely not a long-term actual solution, unless we are truly ready for another American Revolution.

Another proposed solution is the Doctrine of the Lesser Magistrate,[170] which essentially asserts that the states (and other "lesser" in power government officials) need to practice the principle of "interposition" and reclaim their rightful authority. Some state legislatures are seeking to do exactly that and continue to introduce legislation advancing this doctrine.

This is essentially civil disobedience because it is encouraging "defiance" of federal law, and this doctrine asserts that the "lesser" government officials should stand on *legitimate* authority and not simply follow the federal government when that government is acting disobediently to Divine Law. Like any form of civil disobedience, this level of interposition may certainly be viewed as strict defiance, and how successful such interposition can be necessarily depends on how committed the interposer is willing to go to advance this solution.

While a legitimate solution, this doctrine does not comprehensively provide for *every* state (unless each state gets on board), nor does it address issues of federal government overreach into areas we may not immediately consider moral: term limits for the Supreme Court, federal budgeting issues, economics, etc. Certainly some issues are more pressing (such as abortion and same-sex marriage), but it would be error to overlook critical government issues simply because abortion is a *bigger* issue.

Truthfully, there are so many ways that the federal government has overstepped, and it is incumbent upon every true statesmen to do everything we can, especially in proper lawful order if possible, and within every area and issue.

While our situation in government is truly dire, there is still hope, chiefly for the reason that our system is still working, though it is incredibly misdirected and lacking a healthy level of citizen interaction and especially proper education and understanding of what is the original system's design, foundation, and legitimate authority.

At the end of the day, it is evident that the common man and woman, *the people*, still dearly love America and are committed to the foundational principles upon which the Founders built this nation. The Founders themselves realized that there may come a time where amendments to the U.S. Constitution would be necessary, and they specifically provided for that likelihood within the U.S. Constitution itself in Article V so that we have a legitimate *legal basis* to reassert the correct foundation and refocus on the only legitimate role and reason for government: securing our unalienable rights.

It is just as critical today to remember that the Founders did everything they possibly could by way of appealing directly to the government *prior* to civil disobedience. This remains a vitally important reminder for us 225 years later and we cannot be too quick to snub government altogether, as frustrating and dire as the situation is. We need to first attempt to work within the structure actually provided to us by the Founders who were so forward thinking that they gave us the answer to this crisis within the text of the U.S. Constitution itself.

In his Farewell Address, George Washington admonished, "If in the opinion of the people the distribution or modification of the constitutional powers be in any particular wrong, **let it be corrected by an amendment in the way which the Constitution designates**. But let there be no change by usurpation..."[171] (emphasis added).

The Founders could not have been clearer.

This nation still is and must be loved, by all of us, and there are a multitude of reasons we still should feel the deep resonating passion of patriotism for America. Our American boat is not sinking; it's just so far into the dark waters of secular humanism and relativistic morality that we must reorient a moral compass we have long abandoned.

Let it be clear—the America that was founded by the Declaration of Independence of Independence and the U.S. Constitution is worth loving. The America that possessed clear, explicit values and morals and stood for what is right is worth loving. To this end, we should harbor a deep, profound respect and patriotism for our country, as the Founders did before us. The Founders so loved America and the principles of moral law on which she was founded that they fought for her with conviction and commended her with the national motto "In God we Trust."

Many people claim to love America, but they do not truly love America for her values, morals, and principles. These people who say they love America really love themselves. They love what they think American "freedom" is and will give them. They love the secular humanist philosophy and a form of government that appeals to the Sexual Revolution and appeals to the notion that "freedom" somehow means the ability to never be told "you can't" or "that is wrong."

The hidden assumption of this definition of "freedom" is that the U.S. Constitution is truly meaningless. Yet when we actually consider the logical conclusion of this idea, we can see its absurdity. Government authority is a necessity to mankind, to preserve the greater freedoms of each man and woman that are in fact unalienable. But no man, woman, or government is free from the laws of the reality to which we are presented—the scientific and moral construct.

The Founders understood this plainly, and this is what we must understand in order to reclaim our moral foundation and our beloved American ideals of "life, liberty, and the pursuit of happiness."

The Founders believed in our country and its moral basis so completely that they were willing to stake their "lives, fortunes, and our sacred honor." This is loving America!

There is still every reason to be hopeful in our people and our states to change government from within and without. But it starts with education and a clear understanding of the problem that we have discussed here, and not allowing the secular humanist narrative to control the terms of the debate, leaving us soundly defeated before we even make our opening statement.

Murray makes a key observation that signals his concession of the Sovereign and what is truly happening at the Supreme Court at the foundational level. "The Constitution is broken in ways that cannot be fixed even by a sympathetic Supreme Court. Our legal system is increasingly lawless, unmoored from traditional ideas of 'the rule of law.'"[172]

Again, the latter half of this statement is absolutely true, but the first sentence still concedes that the Supreme Court's acting as Sovereign is just a given. We should not wait for a new era of benevolence or a moral majority of justices on the Court who act as Sovereign simply in ways we agree with. This is still fundamentally missing the point—the Social Contract Theory is never a legitimate form of government. Pragmatically, it would only be a matter of time before the majority swings the other way again. This isn't a long-term solution.

So where *do* we go from here? What is the realistic, practical, and *achievable* solution the Founders provided in Article V?

Article V Convention of States

Many of the foremost constitutional experts and lawyers in the country, including attorney and constitutional expert Michael Farris,[173] are proposing to utilize Article V of the U.S. Constitution (the same section that George Washington referred to in the quotation above) and call a Convention of States.

Because of the Supreme Court's blunt refusal to abide by its constitutionally directed limitations on its powers, there are few solutions that would have any actual, lasting effect—including civil disobedience piecemeal within each state. The latter is a genuine and morally correct effort individually as circumstances require, but necessarily cannot encompass a solution on a *national* level to reach government itself.

The Founders foresaw that there might arise a need in future generations to amend the U.S. Constitution in order to continue preserving the sole legitimate form of government (to protect and secure our unalienable rights), and specifically provided for that constitutional remedy. We should listen to the Founders and attempt to follow their guidance and clearly given solution.

Article V of the U.S. Constitution provides:

> *The Congress, whenever two thirds of both Houses shall deem it necessary, shall propose Amendments to the Constitution,*

> **_or_**, *on the Application of two thirds of several States, shall call a Convention for proposing Amendments* (emphasis added).[174]

The idea of a Convention of States is to convene delegates from the states for the specific purpose of proposing amendment(s) to the U.S. Constitution and quelling the constitutional crisis on many key levels.

Per Article V, a Convention may be called in one of two ways: either by the U.S. Congress (having two thirds of both the House and the Senate agree to call a convention), **or** if two-thirds of the states submit an application to convene. If either of these two ways to call a convention occurs, Congress *must* call a Convention of States.

The Convention of States Project[175] is focusing on the second option—submission to Congress the application of two-thirds of the states. An Article V Convention of States through application occurs in five key steps:

1. Application for a Convention of States

Each state legislature must submit *the same* application to the U.S. Congress for a Convention of States for the purpose of proposing amendments. As of 2015, at least 34 state legislatures must submit an application in order to meet the requirement for two-thirds of the states.

The application provides for a very limited scope of what issues may be addressed for Amendments. While some objectors raise concerns that a Convention would become a "runaway" no-holds-barred revamp of the U.S. Constitution or that we are dangerously piercing into the U.S. Constitution, these fears misunderstand the limited authority of the Convention of States.

The current Convention of States project has three key items it encourages states to submit in application. Amendments will be sought which "impose fiscal restraints on the federal government, limit the power and jurisdiction of the federal government, and impose term limits on federal officials."[176] Assuming that 34 states submit these exact issues, the Convention is limited to Amendments addressing those issues. The Convention may limit itself further, but it cannot expand beyond the application issues.

2. Scheduling a time and place for a Convention of States

Once Congress receives the same application from two-thirds of the states, Congress *must* call for a Convention. The language of Article V does not give Congress an option, but rather states that Congress *shall* call a Convention.

Importantly, the term "shall" meant the same directive to the Founder lawyers as it still does to lawyers and to Congress today: mandatory, no option. The Founders specifically used the term *shall* rather than *may* so that Congress must call a Convention of States once the triggering action of application of two-thirds states has been fulfilled.

This is not merely a hope that if the states lobby Congress sufficiently, they will decide to call a Convention. This is mandatory under Article V.

3. Selection of Delegates

Each state then selects its delegates to attend the Convention of States on the individual state's behalf. The process of selecting delegates is up to each individual state (Article V does not prescribe a method by which the states must select their delegates), but at the Convention, each state has only *one* vote—similarly to how each state has one application—regardless of how many delegates are sent to the Convention.

Some objectors to a Convention of States as a solution voice concerns that the most liberal states (California, New York, Michigan, and Vermont) would send an overwhelming number of delegates and overtake the Convention. Under Article V, this is impossible, similarly to California taking over the Senate—the state gets two senators, period. At the Convention of States, each state gets only one vote, regardless of their population or total number of delegates.

4. Convention of States

The Convention of States is then held at the time and place specified by the U.S. Congress, and the delegates from the states attend. The delegates from the states draft and prepare the proposed Constitutional Amendments. Importantly, the proposed amendments must be germane to the subject or subjects specifically listed in the application. This means that the scope of the amendments is *very* limited.

One of the key misunderstandings and therefore concerns of those opposed to a Convention of States solution is the fear of a "runaway" Convention—that once we open the possibility for Constitutional editing, we will have effectively opened Pandora's box. However, we have already seen the Constitution effectively amended by Congressional power through operation of the first clause of Article V and the remainder of the U.S. Constitution is still fully intact. At a Convention of States, each application must be in agreement with and consistent with all other applications on the subject matter. Any issues that are not germane to the application or outside the scope of it cannot be addressed.

The delegates will be carefully instructed by their representative states that they must stay germane and adhere to the subject matter at hand. This will be especially true of the 34 states that will have passed the official applications. Within each application, the state legislatures instruct their delegates to adhere to the subject matter stated in the application. Since a super-majority of delegates will be specifically instructed by their legislature, the other 16 states would effectively be blocked even if a handful with a runaway spirit desired to try an end-run around the applications' specified issues. These checks and balances are far more effective than the current checks on power abuse in Washington, D.C.

Amendments that are approved by a majority of states at the Convention (26 states, as of 2015, if all states participate), are sent to all the State Legislatures for ratification.

5. Ratification of Proposed Amendment(s)

The Convention of States Project seeks more than one amendment. Currently, perhaps as many as six or seven amendments would be proposed limiting various aspects of federal power. These proposed amendments will be sent out as a package like the original Bill of Rights, but must be ratified individually. When 38 state legislatures ratify a particular Amendment sent from the Convention, that Amendment is ratified and becomes and official part of the U.S. Constitution and supreme law.

The Convention of States project is focusing on several key areas for application and proposed amendments:

- A balanced budget amendment
- A redefinition of the General Welfare Clause (the original view was the federal government could not spend money on any topic within the jurisdiction of the states)
- A redefinition of the Commerce Clause (the original view was that Congress was granted a narrow and exclusive power to regulate shipments across state lines—not all the economic activity of the nation)
- A prohibition of using international treaties and law to govern the domestic law of the United States

- A limitation on using Executive Orders and federal regulations to enact laws (since Congress is supposed to be the exclusive agency to enact laws)
- Imposing term limits on Congress and the Supreme Court
- Placing an upper limit on federal taxation
- Requiring the sunset of all existing federal taxes and a super-majority vote to replace them with new, fairer taxes[177]

An Article V Convention of States is exactly what the Founders envisioned during times of constitutional crisis and specifically provided for in Article V, and this option remains the best and most feasible option to deal *constitutionally* with the current crisis.

It is worth genuinely considering that an Article V Convention of States is the very solution provided for by the Founders themselves. This says quite a bit about the legal practicality of this solution and the intent of the Founders for restraining a runaway federal government. We should not take that lightly.

When Hamilton and Madison discussed the U.S. Constitution in the Federalist Papers, they specifically recognized that the U.S. Constitution is a fixed, written document, that it may contain errors or by other necessity require amending to preserve the legitimate role of government, and that Article V is the best process to accomplish that.[178]

Some legal scholars decry the Founding Documents Hierarchy as rooted in Divine Law because of the Founders' permissive slavery, view on women's rights to vote, and other examples. But in addition to being extraordinarily intelligent lawyers, the Founders also approached the U.S. Constitution with a great deal of humility and the specific recognition that they may not have gotten *everything* right. Their goal, however, was squarely premised in Divine Law: that government must function only to secure God-given, unalienable rights.

The Founders provided Article V for two reasons: First, to provide a valid mechanism of amending the U.S. Constitution if corrections must be made; Second, to provide a valid mechanism for reorienting a usurping federal government that is not fulfilling its proper role of securing the people's rights.

These five steps for a Convention of States may seem like a long haul, but the overwhelming majority of states are still largely conservative and Republican. This is important to the states being a key to the solution because although the federal government is a runaway totalitarian Sovereign, the states still hold the power to force Congress to call a Convention of States and actually, meaningfully participate in legitimate restoration of Originalism, state sovereignty, and American values.

This is not simply about gaining a "moral majority." Generally, Christians are entering the debate unwittingly conceding that the foundation of law to be a Social Contract Theory. We have preached that we must reclaim American government through a Christian majority and that if we simply had the majority vote on the Supreme Court, we would reclaim biblical values.

While this may be technically true that a truly moral Supreme Court would be *better* than an amoral majority, this will only help slow down a leaking wall until an amoral majority again takes hold and bursts the dams. We have to understand and articulate that the problem is not what majority opinion is prevailing—the problem is ignoring and misunderstanding our *only* legitimate legal basis in Divine Law authority.

It is irrelevant where on the spectrum the moral majority is situated at any given time or what percentage of Americans are faith-based Christians. It could be 1 percent or 100 percent. What truly matters is the basis of our appeal and the basis of our government's actual legitimate authority.

It's also important to realize that the various proposed solutions are not necessarily mutually exclusive. Christians (and any legal scholar who is actually thinking) agree on the problem: a runaway and usurping federal government. We also agree on the goal: restoring Originalism and restoring the states' powers textually granted by the U.S. Constitution through the Ninth and Tenth Amendments, while limiting the federal government to its actual Constitutional scope of authority.

We are all on the same team here, and we can debate the merits of various proposed solutions, but the debate should focus on what is the most practically and legally viable, comprehensive solution, rather than discord among ourselves over various strict allegiances to proposals. Legally and practically, the best solution is an Article V Convention of States and that is why this solution is offered here comprehensively and the reader is encouraged to get involved in this project within their state and encourage others to understand the problem and this solution.

We are a Divine Law country. There is absolutely no question about that. Our nation was born from a justified revolution through the Declaration of Independence. To become a Social Contract Theory state, we would have to seek and win a full revolution again (which would be an illegitimate revolution because it is against universal, discoverable moral law and an illegitimate "authority" in secular humanism) and become something other than the United States of America and under legal documents other than our Declaration of Independence and U.S. Constitution.

Because the secular humanists know that Divine Law *is* inextricably intertwined with American Civil Government, they shrewdly abused the powers of the only branch of civil government that could not easily be stopped—the Supreme Court. Once the Supreme Court self-proclaimed unfettered power to read into the Supreme Law anything that it desired, we ceased in practicality to be a Divine Law nation, though we still are in actuality.

This was *exactly* the sort of usurpation that Hamilton, Madison, and the other Founder lawyers feared, and why Article V provides a concrete, practical, and achievable solution. As John Adams wrote,

> "While our country remains untainted with the principles and manners which are now producing desolation in so many parts of the world; while she continues sincere, and incapable of insidious and impious policy, we shall have the strongest reason to rejoice in the local destination assigned us by Providence. But should the people of America once become capable of that deep simulation towards one another, and towards foreign nations, which assumes the language of justice and moderation, while it is practicing iniquity and extravagance, and displays in the most captivating manner the charming pictures of candor, frankness, and sincerity, while it is rioting in rapine and insolence, this country will be the most miserable habitation in the world. Because **we have no government, armed with power, capable of contending with human passions, unbridled by morality and religion.** Avarice, ambition, revenge and licentiousness would break the strongest cords of our Constitution, as a whale goes through a net. **Our Constitution was made only for a moral and religious people. It is wholly inadequate to the government of any other. Oaths in this country are as yet universally considered as sacred obligations.** That which you have taken, and so solemnly repeated on that venerable ground, is an ample pledge of your sincerity and devotion to your country and its government."[179]

To fully understand why an Article V Convention of States is necessary, we have to first truly understand the crux of the problem. This solution only makes sense as the *best* solution if the problem itself is correctly identified and attacked for what it is—a rewriting of American foundational history. The Convention of States is the most legally viable solution because the only check on the Supreme Court's power is the U.S. Constitution itself.

No solution rooted in mere majority rule or other manifestations of the Social Contract Theory will work, nor should they. We have to reclaim America's founding principles and Founding Documents Hierarchy.

This effort begins in civil stewardship and education. There are many dedicated, sincere Christians who understand that there is a problem, and we now understand the problem more clearly and why Article V is the best solution.

We have to get involved and educate others. We are failing at educating other Christians on true history and worldview philosophies. We are attacking current events from a Constitutional Law basis and merely accepting the past 50+ years of Supreme Court precedent.

We are losing.

And we are suffering the determinable consequences of a country that is choosing to go against Divine Law. We may not have immediately perceived the consequences back in the 1950s and 1960s, but we are perceiving them now and we must enter the intellectual battleground to reclaim America, understanding the sly tactics that secular humanists wage against us and meet them with the *legal basis* for a moral constitution.

We have to educate ourselves, our churches, and our children on the true history of America and our basis in moral Divine Law. Only then can we, like the Founder lawyers originally did at the

Constitutional Convention, implement a truly successful reclamation of our moral basis to our U.S. Constitution and our Country.

Like the government itself, there may be several ways to implement this, but we have to first be sure that our goal is to restore the proper role of government: to secure the inalienable rights that flow from God and ensure that government abides by Divine Law.

One author summed the problem of education in churches perfectly:

> "Ignoring the problem isn't going to make it go away. We need to equip everyone within the church to face the battle head on. ... We have to face these issues with boldness, clarity, and the full authority of God's Word. While parents are primarily responsible for training children, God also gave the church an essential role in spiritual education (Ephesians 4:11). It's a team effort. Unfortunately, most parents have let the church take it over completely, and the church has failed to equip not only their children but also the parents with a real understanding of how to know, defend, and share their faith. By not teaching apologetics and biblical authority…we are setting up our entire church body for failure. The signs of failure are everywhere. Are we willing to make a conscious change to reverse the decline?"[180]

We also must pray for our country and especially those people who have been pawns of the Sexual Revolution and whose lives will end in regret and tragedy. Only God can change the heart. Government has limited enforcement, but the idea of restorative justice deals with a *heart* change, which necessarily requires morality.

In the aftermath of the *Obergefell* decision, apologist and author Ravi Zacharias tweeted, "What is right has to win the day over what we may see as rights."[181]

We must continue in what is Truth and advocate for legitimate rights and legitimate authority under Divine Law.

We must teach our children the dangers and disturbing truths about the secular humanist agenda and its perversion and pervasiveness in society. The Apostle Paul wrote:

> "But know this, that in the last days perilous times will come: For men will be lovers of themselves, lovers of money, boasters, proud, blasphemers, disobedient to parents, unthankful, unholy, unloving, unforgiving, slanderers, without self-control, brutal, despisers of good, traitors, headstrong, haughty, lovers of pleasure rather than lovers of God, having a form of godliness but denying its power. And from such people turn away!
>
> But you must continue in the things which you have learned and been assured of, knowing from whom you have learned them, and that from childhood you have known the Holy Scriptures, which are able to make you wise for salvation through faith which is in Christ Jesus. All Scripture is given by inspiration of God, and is profitable for doctrine, for reproof, for correction, for instruction in righteousness, that the man of God may be complete, thoroughly equipped for every good work."[182]

Let us become ever more thoroughly equipped to instruct in righteousness and continue in the things that we have learned. We have to be socially *engaged* citizens and take responsibility for our country and its direction in law. Reclaiming the moral basis of U.S. Constitutional interpretation begins with education and understanding these basic truths, and then actively engaging our culture and our government.

Stand firm. Be involved. Teach Truth in love.

*"Providence has given to our people the choice of their
rulers, and it is the duty as well as the privilege
and interest of our Christian nation,
to select and prefer Christians for their rulers."*[183]

- Supreme Court Chief Justice John Jay

BIBLIOGRAPHY

1   John Adams, Military Speech, 1798
2   *Obergefell v. Hodges*, 576 U.S. _____ (2015), 2015 WL 213646
3   *Obergefell v. Hodges*, 576 U.S. _____ (2015), 2015 WL 213646
4   Jean-Paul Sartre, *Imagination: A Psychological Critique*, 1936
5   *Lawrence v. Texas*, 539 U.S. 558 (2003)
6   Denny Burk, *Ending Tax Exemptions Means Ending Churches*, TheFederalist.com, June 19, 2015
7   Letter from John Adams to Thomas Jefferson, September 14, 1813
8   James E. Fleming, Fidelity to Our Imperfect Constitution, pp. 130
9   Christopher Hitchens, *god Is Not Great: How Religion Poisons Everything*
10 Tom Flynn, *Secular Humanism's Unique Selling Proposition*
11 C.S. Lewis, *The Abolition of Man*, pp. 65-67
12 Nancy Pearcey, *Total Truth*, pp. 297-298
13 2 Timothy 3:16-17
14 Nancy Pearcey, *Saving Leonardo*, pp. 1-2
15 Thomas Jefferson, Letter to J. Fishback, 1809
16 James Madison, Letter to William Bradford, September 1773
17 John Adams, Letter to Thomas Jefferson, June 28, 1813
18 George Washington, 1789 Thanksgiving Proclamation
19 George Washington, Farewell Address, 1796
20 Benjamin Rush, Letter to Elias Boundinot, July 9, 1788
21 For a more comprehensive discussion on the Founders' faith, see, e.g. David Barton, *Original Intent* (1996)
22 The term "separation of church and state" appeared n Thomas Jefferson's letter to the Danbury Baptist Ass'n of Danbury, CT (1803)
23 *Obergefell v. Hodges*, 576 U.S. _____ (2015), 2015 WL 213646
24 Text of the 24th Mathew O. Tobriner Memorial Lecture in Constitutional Law presented at the University of California Hastings College of Law, San Francisco, January 12, 2015
25 *Obergefell v. Hodges*, 576 U.S. _____ (2015), 2015 WL 213646
26 *Marbury v. Madison*, 5 U.S. 137 (1803)

27 U.S. Constitution, Article III

28 U.S. Constitution, Article III

29 Jesse Covington, The Supreme Court: Guardian or Threat? (Article, June 8, 2015)

30 U.S. Constitution, Amendment X

31 Alexander Hamilton, Federalist 78: "The judiciary, on the contrary, has no influence over either the sword or the purse; no direction either of the strength or the wealth of the society; and can take no active resolution whatever. It may truly be said to have neither force nor will, but merely judgment; and must ultimately depend upon the aid of the exective arm even for the efficacy of its judgments."

32 *Brown v. Allen*, 344 U.S. 443, 540 (1953)

33 U.S. Constitution, Article III

34 Thomas Paine, *Common Sense* (1776)

35 Roger Sherman, *Correspondence Between Roger Sherman and Samuel Hopkins* (1889), p. 10, from Roger Sherman to Samuel Hopkins, June 28, 1790

36 U.S. Supreme Court, Article III

37 Frederic Bastiat, *The Law*

38 *A Secular Humanist Declaration*, secularhumanism.org, July 29, 2005, accessed July 2015

39 Theodore Schick, Jr. *Morality Requires God … or Does It?* Secularhumanism.org July 2005, accessed July 2015.

40 Francis Schaeffer, *A Christian Manifesto*, 1982

41 Francis Schaeffer, *A Christian Manifesto,* 1982

42 Harold Kushner, *When Bad Things Happen to Good People*, 81 (1981)

43 Francis Schaeffer, *A Christian Manifesto*, 1982

44 Arthur Allen Leff, *Unspeakable Ethics, Unnatural Law*

45 C.S. Lewis, *Mere Christianity*, pp. 1

46 Genesis 1:1 (NKJV)

47 Romans 13:1-6 (NKJV)

48 Alvin Plantinga, *Where the Conflict Really Lies: Science, Religion, and Naturalism*

49 Debate transcript with Richard Taylor, http://www.reasonablefaith.org/debate-transcripts accessed October 2015

50 Richard Taylor, *Ethics, Faith, and Reason*

51 Jean-Jacques Rousseau, *The Social Contract*

52 Nancy Pearcey, *Total Truth*

53 Suzanne Collins, *The Hunger Games Series*, 2008-2010

54 Jean-Jacques Rousseau, *The Social Contract*

55 Philosopher Jean-Paul Sartre, *Essays in Existentialism*

56 Mary Poplin, *Is Reality Secular?*, pp. 105-106

57 Mary Poplin, *Is Reality Secular?*, pp. 57

58   Arthur Allen Leff, *Unspeakable Ethics, Unnatural Law*

59   William Lane Craig, *On Guard*, pp. 30

60   *Roe v. Wade*, 410 U.S. 113 (1973)

61   John Adams in a letter to Thomas Jefferson on June 28, 1813

62   William Lane Craig, *On Guard*, pp. 183

63   Nancy Pearcey, *Total Truth*, pp. 276-279

64   Jefferson's Opinion on the Constitutionality of a National Bank, 1791

65   David Forte, *The Originalist Perspective*

66   Google Dictionary, 2015

67   John Quincy Adams, *An Oration Delivered Before the Inhabitants of the Town of Newburyport at Their Request on the Sixty-First Anniversary of the Declaration of Independence, July 4, 1837* (1837), pp. 5-6

68   Declaration of Independence

69   Declaration of Independence

70   Robert Hole, *The American Declaration of Independence of July 4th, 1776*, History Review Issue 39, March 2001

71   Declaration of Independence

72   Declaration of Independence

73   Declaration of Independence

74   *Black's Law Dictionary*, see, e.g., "unalienable" and "inalienable" (2nd Edition; A.D. 1910 and 8th Edition; A.D. 2004)

75   Declaration of Independence

76   Declaration of Independence

77   Webster's 1828 Dictionary

78   Samuel Adams, Proclamation of a Day of Fast as Governor of Massachusetts, March 20, 1797

79   Federalist 43; James Madison, *Memorial and Remonstrance against Religious Assessments*

80   Romans 13:1 (NKJV)

81   Declaration of Independence

82   Declaration of Independence

83   Declaration of Independence

84   Declaration of Independence

85   Declaration of Independence

86   John M. Mason, *A Collection of the Facts and Documents Relative to the Death of Major General Alexander Hamilton* (1804), p. 53

87   This theory was first widely publicized in 1907 by J. Allen Smith in *The Spirit of American Government: A Study of the Constitution.*

88   Federalist 43; James Madison, *Memorial and Remonstrance against Religious Assessments*

89 Federalist 43; James Madison, *Memorial and Remonstrance against Religious Assessments*

90 James Madison, Federalist No. 51

91 Declaration of Independence

92 Alexander Hamilton, Federalist No. 84

93 Alexander Hamilton, Federalist No. 84

94 *Black's Law Dictionary* (8th Edition; 2004)

95 James Madison, Federalist No. 51

96 James Madison, Letter to James Robertson, April 20, 1831

97 Federalist 43; James Madison, *Memorial and Remonstrance against Religious Assessments*

98 United States House Judiciary Committee of Congress, 1854

99 U.S. Constitution, Preamble

100 James Madison, Address to Congress, June 8, 1789

101 See, e.g. *Resolution of the First Congress Submitting Twelve Amendments to the Constitution* and the National Archives: History of the Bill of Rights

102 Roger Sherman, to Congress 1789

103 John Adams, Letter to Thomas Jefferson, June 28, 1813

104 U.S. Constitution, Amendment I

105 Annals of Congress 439 (1789)

106 U.S. Constitution, Amendment IX

107 U.S. Constitution, Amendment X

108 U.S. Constitution, Article 1, Sec. 8

109 Kentucky State Constitution, Amendment I

110 U.S. Constitution, Article VI

111 *Obergefell v. Hodges*, 576 U.S. _____ (2015), 2015 WL 213646

112 Joseph Story, *A Discourse Pronounced Upon the Inauguration of the Autor as Dane Professor of Law in Harvard University* (1829), pp. 20-21

113 *Griswold v. Connecticut*, 381 U.S. 479 (1965)

114 Merriam-Webster Collegiate Dictionary, 10th Edition, 1996

115 *Griswold v. Connecticut*, 381 U.S. 479 (1965)

116 U.S. Constitution, Amendment X

117 Hans Christian Andersen, The Emperor's New Clothes

118 Ontario Superior Court opinion

119 Pat Miller, Willfully Ignorant, attributed to "Adolf Hitler—Mein Kampf" (pp. 77)

120 John Adams, Letter to John Pitts, 1776

121 John Dickinson, Reply to a Committee in Barbados, 1766

122 *Brown v. Allen*, 344 U.S. 443, 540 (1953)

123 U.S. Constitution, Article V

124 *Bolling v. Sharpe*, 347 U.S. 497 (1954)

125 U.S. Constitution, Amendment I

126 *Everson v. Board of Education*, 330 U.S. 1 (1947)

127 Simone de Beauvior, *The Second Sex*, 1949

128 Mallory Millett, Marxist Feminism's Ruined Lives, (Article on TruthRevolt.
org, Sept. 2014 - http://www.truthrevolt.org/commentary/millett-marxist-
feminisms-ruined-lives#.Vcnft9gNJEB.twitter accessed April 2015)

129 Cleon Skousen, *The Naked Communist*, 1958

130 *Everson v. Board of Education*, 330 U.S. 1, 15-16

131 Library of Congress, also available on its website at http://www.loc.gov/loc/
lcib/9806/danpre.html

132 *Griswold v. Connecticut*, 381 U.S. 479 (1965)

133 U.S. Constitution, Amendment X

134 A good commentary on this general issue is by John M. Walker Jr., *The
Unfortunate Politicization of Judicial Confirmation Hearings*, The Atlantic, July 9,
2012

135 *Lemon v. Kurtzman*, 403 U.S. 602 (1971)

136 Nancy Pearcey, Total Truth, pp.

137 *Roe v. Wade*, 410 U.S. 113 (1973)

138 Katha Pollitt, "How to Really Defend Planned Parenthood," NY Times
Op-Ed, August 5, 2015

139 *Roe v. Wade*, 410 U.S. 113 (1973)

140 Justice Blackmun, qtd. Woodward, Bob "The Abortion Papers," *Washington
Post* (Jan. 22, 1989)

141 *Planned Parenthood v. Casey*, 505 U.S. 833 (1992)

142 Mark Levin, *Ameritopia* (2012)

143 U.S. Constitution, Article IV, Section 4

144 *City of Boerne v. Flores*, 521 U.S. 507 (1997)

145 *Employment Division v. Smith*, 494 U.S. 872 (1990)

146 *Lawrence v. Texas*, 539 U.S. 558 (2003)

147 *Bowers v. Hardwick*, 478 U.S. 186 (1986)

148 *Van Orden v. Perry*, 545 U.S. 677 (2005)

149 *Van Orden v. Perry*, 545 U.S. 677 (2005)

150 *McCreary County v. ACLU of Kentucky*, 545 U.S. 844 (2005)

151 *McCreary County v. ACLU of Kentucky*, 545 U.S. 844 (2005)

152 *Obergefell v. Hodges*, 576 U.S. _____ (2015), 2015 WL 213646

153 Michael Schutt, *The Illegal Trouble with Obergefell*, Journal of Worldview
Academy, August 1, 2015

154 Benjamin Franklin, Speech to the Constitutional Convention, 1787

155 Francis Schaeffer, Address at the University of Notre Dame, April 1981

156 C.S. Lewis, Mere Christianity, pp. 1

157 Nancy Pearcey, Total Truth, pp. 299

158 C.S. Lewis, Mere Christianity, pp. 2

159 Bryan Beauman, "Should we Legislate Morality?" (Answers Magazine, July 1, 2014)

160 Romans 1:19-20 (NLT)

161 Psalm 19:1 (KJV)

162 Noah Webster, Writings to James Madison, October 16, 1829

163 Noah Webster, Preface to The American Dictionary of the English Language, 1828

164 Focus on the Family, "Americans Are More Divided Over Same-Sex Marriage; Want Religious Liberty Protections," 2015

165 U.S. Constitution, Amendment I

166 Canadian Court, Loyola, para 47

167 Washington's Farewell Address, 1796

168 Charles Murray, By The People, (Introduction, xiii)

169 American Principles Project, Oct. 8, 2015, https://americanprinciplesproject. org/founding-principles/statement-calling-for-constitutional-resistance-to-obergefell-v-hodges%E2%80%AF/ accessed October 8, 2015.

170 See, The Doctrine of the Lesser Magistrates, Matt Trewhella (2013)

171 Washington's Farewell Address, 1796

172 Charles Murray, By The People

173 Michael Farris, Esq., constitutional attorney and national director of the Convention of States project, contributed largely to the content in Chapter 13

174 U.S. Constitution, Article V

175 More information on the Convention of States project can be found at www. conventionofstates.com

176 Language of the applications suggested by Convention of States Project

177 Convention of States Project via www.conventionofstates.com

178 See, e.g. Federalists 43 and 85

179 John Adams, Letter to the Officers of the First Brigade of the Third Division of the Militia of Massachusetts, October 11, 1798, qtd. in Revolutionary Services and Civil Life of General William Hull (1848), pp 265-6.

180 Nate Loper, "The Church—Training Ground for Truth," AiG.org January 1, 2013

181 Ravi Zacharias, personal Twitter page, July 2015

182 2 Timothy 3:1-5,14-17 (NKJV)

183 Letter to John Murray (12 October 1816) as published in The Life of John Jay (1833) by William Jay, Vol. 2, p. 376